ADVOCACY GROUPS

Published in association with the Centre for Canadian Studies at Mount Allison University. Information on the Canadian Democratic Audit project can be found at www.CanadianDemocraticAudit.ca.

Advisory Group

Titles

John Courtney, *Elections*
William Cross, *Political Parties*
Elisabeth Gidengil, André Blais, Neil Nevitte, and Richard Nadeau, *Citizens*
Jennifer Smith, *Federalism*
Lisa Young and Joanna Everitt, *Advocacy Groups*
David Docherty, *Legislatures*
Graham White, *Cabinets and First Ministers*
Darin Barney, *Communications Technology*
Ian Greene, *The Courts*

ADVOCACY GROUPS

Lisa Young and Joanna Everitt

UBCPress

15 14 13 12 11 10 09 08 07 06 05 04   5 4 3 2 1

Printed in Canada on acid-free paper that is 100% post-consumer recycled, processed chlorine-free, and printed with vegetable-based, low-VOC inks.

Library and Archives Canada Cataloguing in Publication
Young, Lisa
    Advocacy groups / Lisa Young and Joanna Everitt.

(Canadian democratic audit ; 5)
Includes bibliographical references and index.
ISBN 0-7748-1101-3 (set). – ISBN 0-7748-1110-2

1. Pressure groups – Canada. I. Everitt, Joanna Marie, 1964- II. Title. III. Series.

JL186.5.Y68 2004   322.4'3'0971   C2004-904859-7

Canada

UBC Press gratefully acknowledges the financial support for our publishing program of the Government of Canada through the Book Publishing Industry Development Program (BPIDP), and of the Canada Council for the Arts and the British Columbia Arts Council.

The Centre for Canadian Studies thanks the Harold Crabtree Foundation for its support of the Canadian Democratic Audit project.

This book has been published and with the help of the K.D. Srivastava Fund.

UBC Press
The University of British Columbia
2029 West Mall
Vancouver, BC V6T 1Z2
604-822-5959 / Fax: 604-822-6083
www.ubcpress.ca

CONTENTS

Tables

FOREWORD

This volume is part of the Canadian Democratic Audit series. The objective of this series is to consider how well Canadian democracy is performing at the outset of the twenty-first century. In recent years, political and opinion leaders, government commissions, academics, citizen groups, and the popular press have all identified a "democratic deficit" and "democratic malaise" in Canada. These characterizations often are portrayed as the result of a substantial decline in Canadians' confidence in their democratic practices and institutions. Indeed, Canadians are voting in record low numbers, many are turning away from the traditional political institutions, and a large number are expressing declining confidence in both their elected politicians and the electoral process.

Nonetheless, Canadian democracy continues to be the envy of much of the rest of the world. Living in a relatively wealthy and peaceful society, Canadians hold regular elections in which millions cast ballots. These elections are largely fair, efficient, and orderly events. They routinely result in the selection of a government with no question about its legitimate right to govern. Developing democracies from around the globe continue to look to Canadian experts for guidance in establishing electoral practices and democratic institutions. Without a doubt, Canada is widely seen as a leading example of successful democratic practice.

Given these apparently competing views, the time is right for a comprehensive examination of the state of Canadian democracy. Our purposes are to conduct a systematic review of the operations of Canadian democracy, to listen to what others have to say about Canadian democracy, to assess its strengths and weaknesses, to consider where there are opportunities for advancement, and to evaluate popular reform proposals.

A democratic audit requires the setting of benchmarks for evaluation of the practices and institutions to be considered. This necessarily involves substantial consideration of the meaning of democracy. "Democracy" is a contested term and we are not interested here in striking a definitive definition. Nor are we interested in a theoretical model applicable to all parts of the world. Rather we are interested in identifying democratic benchmarks relevant to Canada in the twenty-first century. In selecting these we were guided by the issues raised in the current literature on Canadian democratic practice and by the concerns commonly raised by opinion leaders and found in public opinion data. We have settled on three benchmarks: public participation, inclusiveness, and responsiveness. We believe that any contemporary definition of Canadian democracy must include institutions and decision-making practices that are defined by public participation, that this participation must include all Canadians, and that government outcomes must respond to the views of Canadians.

While settling on these guiding principles, we have not imposed a strict set of democratic criteria on all of the evaluations that together constitute the Audit. Rather, our approach allows the auditors wide latitude in their evaluations. While all auditors keep the benchmarks of participation, inclusiveness, and responsiveness central to their examinations, each adds additional criteria of particular importance to the subject he or she is considering. We believe this approach of identifying unifying themes, while allowing for divergent perspectives, enhances the project by capturing the robustness of the debate surrounding democratic norms and practices.

We decided at the outset to cover substantial ground and to do so in a relatively short period. These two considerations, coupled with a desire to respond to the most commonly raised criticisms of the contemporary practice of Canadian democracy, result in a series that focuses on public institutions, electoral practices, and new phenomena that are likely to affect democratic life significantly. The series includes volumes that examine key public decision-making bodies: legislatures, the courts, and cabinets and government. The structures of our democratic system are considered in volumes devoted to questions of federalism and the electoral system. The ways in which citizens participate in electoral politics and policy making are a crucial component of the project, and thus we include studies of advocacy groups and political parties. The desire and capacity of Canadians for meaningful participation in public life is also the subject of a volume. Finally, the challenges and opportunities raised by new communication technologies are also considered. The Audit does not include studies devoted to the status of particular groups of Canadians. Rather than separate out Aboriginals, women, new Canadians, and others, these groups are treated together with all Canadians throughout the Audit.

In all, this series includes nine volumes examining specific areas of Canadian democratic life. A tenth, synthetic volume provides an overall assessment and makes sense out of the different approaches and findings found in the rest of the series. Our examination is not exhaustive. Canadian democracy is a vibrant force, the status of which can never be fully captured at one time. Nonetheless the areas we consider involve many of the pressing issues currently facing democracy in Canada. We do not expect to have the final word on this subject. Rather, we hope to encourage others to pursue similar avenues of inquiry.

A project of this scope cannot be accomplished without the support of many individuals. At the top of the list of those deserving credit are the members of the Canadian Democratic Audit team. From the very beginning, the Audit has been a team effort. This outstanding group of academics has spent many hours together, defining the scope of the project, prodding each other on questions of Canadian democracy, and most importantly, supporting one another throughout the endeavour, all with good humour. To Darin Barney, André Blais, Kenneth Carty, John Courtney, David Docherty, Joanna Everitt, Elisabeth Gidengil, Ian Greene, Richard Nadeau, Neil Nevitte, Richard Sigurdson, Jennifer Smith, Frank Strain, Michael Tucker, Graham White, and Lisa Young I am forever grateful.

The Centre for Canadian Studies at Mount Allison University has been my intellectual home for several years. The Centre, along with the Harold Crabtree Foundation, has provided the necessary funding and other assistance necessary to see this project through to fruition. At Mount Allison University, Peter Ennals provided important support to this project when others were skeptical; Wayne MacKay and Michael Fox have continued this support since their respective arrivals on campus; and Joanne Goodrich and Peter Loewen have provided important technical and administrative help.

The University of British Columbia Press, particularly its senior acquisitions editor, Emily Andrew, has been a partner in this project from the very beginning. Emily has been involved in every important decision and has done much to improve the result. Camilla Gurdon has overseen the copyediting and production process and in doing so has made these books better. Scores of Canadian and international political scientists have participated in the project as commentators at our public conferences, as critics at our private meetings, as providers of quiet advice, and as referees of the volumes. The list is too long to name them all, but David Cameron, Sid Noel, Leslie Seidle, Jim Bickerton, Alexandra Dobrowolsky, Livianna Tossutti, Janice Gross Stein, and Frances Abele all deserve special recognition for their contributions. We are also grateful to the Canadian Study of Parliament Group, which partnered with us for our inaugural conference in Ottawa in November 2001.

Finally, this series is dedicated to all of the men and women who contribute to the practice of Canadian democracy. Whether as active participants in parties, groups, courts, or legislatures, or in the media and the universities, without them Canadian democracy would not survive.

William Cross
Director, The Canadian Democratic Audit
Sackville, New Brunswick

ACKNOWLEDGMENTS

While many authors profess that their book would not have been written without the assistance or inspiration of some individual, in our case this is demonstrably true. Had it not been for the leadership demonstrated by Bill Cross in conceiving and executing the Democratic Audit series, neither of the authors of this volume would ever have tackled the project of writing a book about the role of advocacy groups in Canadian politics.

We discovered that auditing as large, amorphous, and unresearched a category as advocacy groups was an extraordinarily challenging task. Given these difficulties, we are particularly grateful to Bill, the members of the advisory group that he assembled, and the other authors of volumes in this series for their input and guidance in constructing our study. While we received sage advice from many, the contributions of Richard Sigurdson, Elisabeth Gidengil, and R.K. Carty particularly stand out. As always, our editor Emily Andrew of UBC Press offered excellent guidance at crucial moments.

We also benefited tremendously from excellent research assistance from John Roslinski, Angela Gallant, and Jason Roy. Camilla Gurdon and the other members of the editorial team at UBC Press made our manuscript a much better document than it would have been otherwise.

Data analysed in the book come from the 2000 Canada Election Study, which was conducted by the Institute for Social Research, York University. The principal investigators were André Blais, Elisabeth Gidengil, Richard Nadeau, and Neil Nevitte. Neither the ISR nor the principal investigators are responsible for the analysis or interpretations of data presented in this book. The book also uses data from the 1981, 1990, and 2000 World Values Surveys, principal investigators Ronald Inglehart and Neil Nevitte.

Joanna Everitt would like to thank all of those individuals who patiently accepted delays on other projects to allow for the completion of this book. She would also like to thank members of her department along with other colleagues at UNBSJ for their support, friendship and encouragement in this and other efforts. As always, she thanks her family for their love and their continued faith in her endeavours.

Lisa Young wishes to thank the Killam Trust for a research fellowship in fall of 2003 that was intended to aid in the completion of other projects but was nonetheless of great assistance in completing this manuscript. She also wishes to thank her son David, who held off his arrival in the world just long enough to allow her to attend the first meeting of the audit group by telephone, her son Joshua, whose imminent arrival focused her mind on completing a draft manuscript in record time, and her husband, Mike Griffin, who shouldered far more than his fair share of myriad domestic tasks while this book was being written and who periodically reminded us of what auditors are supposed to do.

ADVOCACY GROUPS

ADVOCACY GROUPS AND CANADIAN DEMOCRACY

1

Governments touch the lives of every Canadian in a variety of ways. In the modern era of the extensive state, governments do not just determine whether there will be a stop light at a busy intersection. They also decide, for example, what children will learn in school, whether we can have speedy access to life-saving medical treatments, and what kind of toxic substances industries can release into the environment. The pervasive character of government makes it inevitable that most of us will at some point want to influence the direction of a government decision. This desire is often driven by self-interest. Many of us are drawn into political activity in an effort to make government provide a service, like a medical treatment or a new school in our neighbourhood, that we or members of our families need. In other instances, the desire to affect government decisions can be driven by values or a conception of the public interest. Much activism is motivated by a desire to change government policies to concord with our personal beliefs. Indeed, a great many Canadians have been motivated to political action simply by a sense of outrage over governments' actions or inactions.

When a Canadian wants to encourage a government to do something – change a policy, repeal a law, or just leave well enough alone – what can he or she do? A citizen can certainly act as an individual, by contacting his or her elected representative, trying to get media attention, and even participating in government consultation processes. But lone voices are often lost in conversations about public policy, so many of us try to band together with others who share our concern.

Groups may be heard when individuals are not, and groups allow individuals to pool their resources to make their case more forcefully. Consequently, various kinds of advocacy groups have become the predominant way in which citizens interact with governments to try to influence public policy.

In fact, the majority of Canadians perceive groups to be a more effective way of achieving policy change than the traditional method – joining a political party. A recent survey asked, "Which do you think is a more effective way to work for change nowadays: joining a political party or an interest group?" Fully 70 percent of those surveyed replied that groups were more effective (Howe and Northrup 2000).

Canadians' confidence in the effectiveness of groups reflects rapid growth in the number of advocacy groups active in Canada over the past forty years, and the increasing influence groups have come to have on public policy processes. Taken together, these developments make advocacy groups important players in Canadian democracy. Groups are positioned to act as intermediaries between society and government, providing a channel through which citizens can communicate with and try to influence government. This conduit is crucial in a democratic system, so any audit of Canadian democracy must include an examination of how well groups are performing this function.

Our assessment of the performance of groups is informed by our conception of the role groups should ideally play in a liberal democracy. In this ideal, groups are highly participatory, internally democratic organizations that give a large number of citizens a way to engage with governments. Groups should represent the diversity of the society from which they emerge, and should even compensate for some of the representational failures of political parties, legislatures, and executives. Group mobilization should provide a public voice for all relevant interests, not just those that already have influence. And, without surrendering their capacity to govern in the public interest, governments should welcome groups into the policy process and recognize the value of their intermediary capacities.

This ideal conception of the role groups can play leads us to ask the following questions in our audit:

* Who participates in these groups? What form does this participation take?
* How representative are groups of their members, and of the constituencies they claim to represent?

* Which interests are "organized in" and which are not?
* Who is heard? Do some groups experience more difficulty gaining access to decision makers than others? Do some groups consistently win while others lose?
* What tactics do groups employ? Are these harmful to democratic debate in any way?

Taken as a whole, the answers to these questions allow us to gauge the extent to which Canadian advocacy groups contribute to the quality of democracy in Canada.

What Are Advocacy Groups?

When we talk about the role of advocacy groups in the Canadian political process, it is not self-evident what kinds of organizations are included. We deliberately avoid the term "interest group," even though many groups classify themselves that way. The term implies that a group is lobbying government to take an action that benefits its members, financially or otherwise. While this is frequently the case, the label of "interest group" is less suited to groups that lobby government to do something they believe in, like banning abortion or taking action to save an endangered species. We prefer the term "advocacy group" as it encompasses groups acting for the best interests of members as well as groups acting to promote their opinions on an issue in which they do not have a direct interest.

In an effort to make our inquiry as comprehensive as possible, we have opted for a broad and relatively simple definition for advocacy groups: *any organization that seeks to influence government policy, but not to govern.* This distinguishes advocacy groups from political parties, which seek to influence government policy by governing, or at least by trying to elect candidates to legislatures. This definition of an advocacy group would include an organization formed by two or three individuals who live on the same street and are lobbying their municipal government to install a stop sign, as well as a group like the Council of Canadians, which claims thousands of members and lobbies government on issues ranging from the environment to national sovereignty. It also includes industry associations and business lobby groups.

We will, however, distinguish between advocacy groups motivated by self-interest and those acting in support of their view of the public interest. Although the difference between the two types of group is obviously not absolute (and may be swayed by one's sympathies), nonetheless a meaningful distinction can be drawn between the Canadian Pharmaceutical Association or the Canadian Bankers' Association, on the one hand, and Greenpeace or the Canadian Taxpayers Federation, on the other. The two former groups represent industries that lobby government to further their members' pecuniary interests. The two latter organizations are working toward policy objectives, like cleaner air and lower taxes, that may well serve their own personal interests but also represent their conception of the public interest. Perhaps the clearest way to differentiate between these two types of groups is to look to the kinds of benefits each group seeks. The pharmaceutical and bankers' associations are seeking to achieve *selective* benefits, or benefits that apply only to their members. Greenpeace and the Canadian Taxpayers Federation are seeking *collective* benefits, or benefits that are shared by all even if they are not necessarily supported by all. However, while both groups are driven by a set of social and political values, the CTF seeks tax changes that have greater benefit for some segments of society than others. This example shows that even "public interest groups" can seek partially selective benefits under the guise of pursuing their vision of the public interest. In short, though there is no easy means of creating watertight categories of groups, the basic principle of benefit remains significant.

The distinction between groups seeking selective benefits and those seeking collective benefits is important from the perspective of democracy. If only those groups seeking selective benefits are able to find a voice in policy debates, then advocacy group involvement does little to further a democratic discussion of the common interest. There is a school of thought, commonly referred to as pluralism, that holds that the pursuit of selective benefits by competing groups produces outcomes that approximate the public interest. This view assumes that all relevant interests are able to mobilize on an equal footing, and that governments are neutral arbitrators among groups. In our view, neither of these assumptions is empirically founded. Pluralism is discussed in greater detail in Chapter 2.

Our simple definition of an advocacy group also takes into account a peculiar phenomenon: organizations that are not created to influence government sometimes act like advocacy groups. For example, many Canadian churches have lobbied the federal government to assume responsibility for lawsuits stemming from residential schools for Aboriginal people, as the churches claim that these lawsuits may bankrupt them. Because universities rely heavily on public funding, they regularly send representatives to lobby government for increased funding. Similarly, businesses frequently lobby government to make decisions that are favourable to the business's particular needs. While we do not ignore the role that businesses and other institutions play in lobbying government, the central focus of this study is advocacy groups proper – those groups that are formulated specifically with an intent to influence government.

An emerging phenomenon in public administration forces us to further clarify the circumstances under which groups should be considered advocacy groups. This phenomenon is a growing tendency for governments to rely on "third sector," or nongovernmental organizations, to deliver programs. When groups are delivering services on behalf of government, they are not advocacy groups. However, these groups may on occasion seek to influence government policy on matters related to their area of service delivery. Under these circumstances, they are advocacy groups and fall within our definition. For example, the Red Cross delivers services for government by collecting donated blood and blood products and making them available to hospitals, but the organization also seeks to influence government on issues including regulation of the blood supply. In this latter respect, we would consider it an advocacy group. Similarly, charitable organizations may devote most of their efforts to delivering services of some kind, but may also try to influence government policy in related areas. Food banks, for instance, exist mainly to collect and distribute food to Canadians in need. But this activity gives their directors intimate knowledge of the causes and consequences of poverty, which may inspire them to lobby government on issues such as minimum wage laws or social assistance benefits. To the extent that these organizations engage in such advocacy activity, they fall within our definition of advocacy groups.

Our broad definition of advocacy groups – any group that seeks to influence public policy, but not to govern – encompasses a particular subset of organizations that require special attention: social movements. These are best understood as informal networks of groups and individuals sharing a common vision for social and political change. The organizations that are part of social movement networks are sometimes formulated strictly as advocacy groups (i.e., lobbying government for policy change), but are also sometimes focused on encouraging social change. For example, the environmental movement is an extensive network of organizations that share the common objective of trying to protect the environment. Some groups lobby government in pursuit of these goals, while others focus on trying to change peoples' ideas or actions through education. We can imagine any number of small groups that encourage people to ride their bicycles rather than driving. These groups might work with employers to install bike lockers or showers for their employees, but they do not lobby government for policy changes. The environmental movement also includes many individuals who may not belong to any of its organizations, but who consider themselves environmentalists, share the objectives of the movement, and try to protect the environment through their actions (such as recycling, or not driving a car). Thus social movements are more than just advocacy groups.

Several social movements are prominent on the Canadian political scene, including the environmental movement, the women's movement, and the gay and lesbian movement. A "family values" movement has also emerged in direct reaction to the latter two movements. Gaining significance in recent years is the antiglobalization movement, which has a global rather than national focus, and which seeks to limit the power of international capital. The full range of social movement activity is beyond the scope of our audit, which is already broad. Rather, we limit our focus to those organizations within social movements that act like other advocacy groups in trying to influence government policy in some way. This limitation is not meant to imply, however, that the other aspects of social movement activity are less significant to Canadian democracy.

Advocacy groups employ a range of tactics in their quest to influence government decisions. These tactics can be ranged on a spectrum from formal to informal, or traditional to nontraditional. At the formal end of the spectrum are activities such as meeting with cabinet ministers, mayors, public servants, and legislators, presenting briefs to legislative committees, and attending government-sponsored consultation sessions for stakeholders in a particular policy field. At the informal end of the spectrum lie activities such as rallies and protests, signing petitions, holding sit-ins, or engaging in civil disobedience. Some groups, like business organizations, usually limit themselves to tactics from the formal end of the spectrum. Other groups employ a diverse set of tactics, sometimes even attending meetings with influential officials on the same day that they hold large public demonstrations.

By a conservative estimate, there are tens of thousands of advocacy groups in Canada. Some are venerable institutions with lengthy histories, and others spring up for a few months and then disband. Some boast thousands of members, and others only a handful. Some are highly professionalized, with paid staffs and permanent offices, while others are run by volunteers from their homes in their spare time. Clearly, an audit of such a large, amorphous, and diverse set of organizations is a daunting task, and inevitably we have had to narrow our focus to some extent. This book does not try to catalogue all the groups active in Canadian politics, nor are we able to generalize based on any comprehensive survey of these groups. Rather, we focus selectively on a number of higher-profile national groups, while still trying to demonstrate the diversity of advocacy groups in the examples we employ.

The Audit Approach

We have found the task of auditing Canadian advocacy groups extraordinarily challenging. While our colleagues auditing legislatures, executives, and political parties have been able to focus on a limited number of organizations or institutions, we have had to try to make sense of the activities of tens of thousands of organizations operating at the local, provincial, and national levels. Compounding our difficulties, no comprehensive surveys have been conducted in Canada of advocacy groups or their members. It is therefore impossible to draw definitive conclusions about the character of Canadian advocacy groups and what they do.

In the absence of comprehensive surveys, we have compiled an extensive collection of more limited studies, case studies of particular groups and consultation processes, and even media accounts of group activity. From this, we have tried to gain as thorough an understanding as possible of how Canadian advocacy groups organize themselves, what they do, and how they engage with government. We recognize that this method is less than ideal, and our conclusions are consequently often tentative.

As an aside, one of the conclusions we have reached while performing our audit is that Canadian political science research has barely scraped the surface of studying advocacy groups. There is a pressing need for large-scale studies of Canadian advocacy groups, particularly those operating at the provincial and local levels. Understanding of the scope and role of advocacy groups would be greatly enhanced by a wide-ranging effort to catalogue and classify the groups active in a number of sectors, and to examine their forms of internal organization and their tactics. Understanding of the mobilization of groups would be aided by surveys of groups members focusing on their motivations for joining, the scope and extent of their activism, and their assessments of group activity.

We found it particularly difficult to generalize regarding interactions between advocacy groups and Canadian governments. Advocacy groups interact not only with the federal government in Ottawa but also with ten provincial and three territorial governments, as well as a multitude of municipal governments. Some of these governments are very open to interaction with advocacy groups while others are almost entirely closed to it. Complicating matters further, profound variations exist within governments, with some departments amenable to advocacy group input and others opposed to it. Instead of drawing comprehensive conclusions, therefore, we attempt to identify the conditions under which advocacy group-government interactions embody desirable democratic values. In identifying these conditions and "best practices" we hope to give some insight into the potential for democratically beneficial interactions between groups and government.

Our Audit addresses a range of issues pertaining to the scope of citizen involvement in group politics, the openness of the political system to group involvement, the mobilization of bias through the advocacy group system, and the extent to which groups compete with the institutions of representative democracy. All of these questions relate in some way to the Canadian Democratic Audit criteria of participation, responsiveness, and inclusiveness.

PARTICIPATION

The Audit value of participation is centrally important to our evaluation of how advocacy groups contribute to Canadian democracy. Among the benefits advocacy groups can offer to democratic life, the ability to mobilize citizens to participate in the political system is high on the list. Citizen participation requires organization, and groups are one of the most visible means through which citizens can participate. Following from this, we also anticipate that participating in advocacy groups may strengthen citizens' democratic values. That said, there are concerns that groups may mobilize "too much" participation, or participation that takes a corrosive form. Our consideration of participation must take into account three different aspects: extent, equality, and quality.

If we accept that democracy is strengthened by widespread citizen involvement, then it follows that the more citizens who are mobilized into advocacy group activism, the better democracy is served. To study the *extent* of group participation, we analyze data from surveys of the Canadian public to estimate how many Canadians are active in advocacy groups. To put this into perspective, we compare this to the number of Canadians active in political parties and to rates of advocacy group participation in other industrialized countries.

One of the great concerns regarding advocacy group activity from the perspective of democracy is that it furthers a "mobilization of bias" by providing another route through which societal elites – the affluent, the well-educated, members of majority groups – can voice their concerns, while others are left without representation. Alternatively, some groups specifically mobilize politically underrepresented groups such as the poor, women, or Aboriginals; does this balance the picture? To measure the *equality* of participation in Canadian advocacy groups, we compare the demographic breakdown of the population involved in group activity to that of the population not involved.

More than just the quantity of citizen participation must be considered; the *quality* of participation is also key. Those who argue that advocacy groups can contribute to the quality of democracy assume that group members become active participants in the political process by attending group meetings, participating in the group's internal decision making, and being involved in the group's advocacy activities. Is this in fact the case, or do most group members participate simply by offering financial support? We use survey data to determine the percentage of group members who actively attend meetings or spend time working for a group's cause. We also examine the internal structures of a variety of groups to determine what opportunities they offer for citizens to participate.

One of the arguments offered in support of the role of advocacy groups in mobilizing citizen participation holds that such participation instils support for democracy and democratic values. To test this in the Canadian experience, we again use survey data to determine whether citizens who are members of advocacy groups have higher levels of trust in government, are more inclined to believe that they can affect government decision making, and are more inclined to participate in other facets of democratic life such as voting.

RESPONSIVENESS

The Audit criterion of responsiveness has two distinct aspects in the context of advocacy groups. The first dimension is how responsive the groups themselves are, both to their members and to the broader constituency they purport to represent. The second dimension is the responsiveness of government to the interests articulated by groups. This is not to suggest that government should try to accede to all demands made by all groups; rather, the question is how open Canadian governments are to meaningful input from groups, and in what ways they organize group input.

The extent to which advocacy groups contribute to democracy is determined in part by the degree of internal democracy in the groups. Groups contribute to citizens' experience with democracy only if they conduct their internal affairs in accordance with the basic principles of democracy. In this respect, we can evaluate groups in terms of the democratic ideals of equal participation of members, opportunity for members to influence decisions, and representative internal structures (such as election of officers). Beyond this, there is the question of the extent to which groups are responsive to the views of the broader constituencies they purport to represent. If a group claims to speak for "taxpayers" or "women," then its positions and objectives should demonstrate some responsiveness to the views of these people. We examine selected groups to identify the mechanisms that allow them to hear from and respond to the views of their broader constituencies.

The second dimension of responsiveness as it relates to advocacy groups has to do with the openness of Canadian governments to group influence. This does not imply that the democratic ideal we are measuring against is one in which governments acquiesce to as many group demands as possible. Rather, the democratic ideal is that all groups are able to receive a fair hearing, be it in a consultation process, a parliamentary committee, or on the streets. To gauge the responsiveness of Canadian governments we examine the various ways groups interact with governments, with particular emphasis on the opportunities created for groups to present their views to government decision makers. Given that the number of Canadian advocacy groups has proliferated in recent decades, we would expect to see an improvement in the access of groups to decision making over the past thirty or forty years. To the extent that we find the reverse to be true (for example if we find evidence that groups' ability to engage in legal protest activities has been curtailed), we conclude that responsiveness is in decline.

INCLUSIVENESS

The third Audit criterion, inclusiveness, is particularly relevant to advocacy groups, as we have noted the potential for groups to compensate for the representational failures of other institutions (see Docherty 2004; White 2005). The above discussion of participation outlines our benchmarks for determining whether groups are inclusive in their mobilization of citizens. Beyond this, we pay particular attention to the activities of groups that represent previously excluded collectivities of Canadians when we examine the ability of groups to mobilize access to government.

We also consider the inclusiveness of the advocacy group system as a whole. Inclusiveness requires that all relevant identities be given voice in the public sphere. One of the concerns raised by critics of advocacy groups relates to the potential for some interests to be "organized in" to political decision making, while others remain unorganized and therefore unheard. This aspect of advocacy group activity is difficult to measure comprehensively. To attempt to determine the extent to which this is the case, we examine a series of case studies of policy making to see which relevant interests were represented, and which were not.

Plan of the Book

Chapter 2 provides an overview of theoretical perspectives on the role of advocacy groups in democratic political systems and identifies ways in which we might expect advocacy groups to contribute to and detract from the quality of democratic life. In Chapter 3, we turn our attention to the question of who participates in Canadian advocacy groups, and Chapter 4 considers what kinds of participatory opportunities Canadian advocacy groups offer to citizens. Chapter 5 looks at the question of which interests tend to mobilize and which do not find a voice in the advocacy group system. Chapters 6 and 7 examine the ways in which advocacy groups try to make their voices heard, ranging from protests in the streets to high-powered private lobbying. The related question of which interests tend to prevail in influencing government policy forms the focus of Chapter 8. Finally, Chapter 9 summarizes our findings and makes recommendations both for groups and for governments, with a view to maximizing the contribution advocacy groups make to the quality of democracy in Canada.

Before moving to the substance of the Audit, it is necessary to take a broader look at the potential for advocacy groups to contribute to Canadian democracy. This is a matter of some controversy, among both citizens and observers of politics. To set the stage for our audit, we turn now to an examination of these competing views of the role of advocacy groups.

PERSPECTIVES ON ADVOCACY GROUPS AND DEMOCRACY

2

Democratic political systems create the necessary preconditions for advocacy groups to emerge because they guarantee freedom of expression and association, both of which are essential to advocacy group functioning. In democratic systems where governments are open to – and may even desire – citizen input into the policy process, individuals have strong incentives to band together to put forward their views or protect their interests. In all the democratic political systems where the preconditions for advocacy group formation are in place, advocacy groups have formed. Although the extent and the specific character of group mobilization vary from country to country, advocacy groups are an integral part of the political process in modern democracies.

The role of advocacy groups in modern democracies is, however, highly contentious. While some observers see advocacy groups as necessary to vibrant democratic life, others perceive them as corrosive forces championing special interests over the common interest. In this chapter, we set out our definition of an advocacy group and then outline the debate over the role of advocacy groups in democracy.

How Can Advocacy Groups Contribute to Democracy?

When political scientists – all of them American – first began to study the role played by interest groups in democratic systems, what emerged was a school of thought arguing that interest groups were beneficial, and even necessary, to modern democracy (Truman 1951; Lindblom 1963; Dahl 1961). This perspective, pluralism, proceeds from the assumptions that political power is dispersed among political institutions and interest groups, and that different people have different kinds of power in different issue areas. Citizens have myriad interests, and pluralists assert that citizens can expect on some issues to be on the winning side, and on others to be on the losing side. The state does not favour some interests over others in a systematic manner, because government is viewed as merely a neutral arena in which groups compete. The political system envisioned by the pluralists has no consistent winners or losers. In this worldview, competition among groups for policy outcomes yields political stability and an approximation of the public good.

The pluralist view of interest groups has been criticized on a number of fronts. One common criticism focuses on the factual basis for the assertion that all interests are potentially equal and that there are no consistent winners under pluralist arrangements. As E.E. Schattschneider (1960, 35) asserted, "The chorus [in the pluralist heaven] sings with a strong upper-class accent." Many critics believe the pluralist view ignored the persistent influence of business in American democracy and served to support and legitimize this state of affairs. In its construction, the pluralist argument has much in common with defences of laissez-faire economics. But as political theorist Jane Mansbridge (1992, 35) argued, "The argument for pure laissez-faire works no better in the modern polity than in the modern economy. A laissez-faire economy inevitably creates monopolies and oligopolies, whose immense power must be regulated to limit intolerable distortions of the market. Similarly ... the most powerful organized interests often look no more like the textbook citizen-initiated voluntary association than General Motors looks like a ma-and-pa store."

However, it is possible to construct an argument in favour of advocacy group participation in democratic political life that avoids some of the pitfalls of pluralism. At the heart of this argument is the idea that advocacy groups contribute to democracy by providing a channel through which citizens can connect with the state. When such representative institutions as political parties or legislatures are unable to articulate the views or interests of a particular group, the advocacy group route allows citizens to mobilize in order to make their voices heard. To the extent that parties and legislatures systematically underrepresent segments of the population, this route is all the more important. More specifically, five functions of advocacy groups have the potential to contribute to the quality of democracy:

1 giving voice to citizen interests, particularly those not represented in mainstream institutions
2 providing a route through which citizens can participate
3 supporting the development and maintenance of a culture of democracy
4 facilitating the development of better public policy
5 making government more responsive to citizens.

Groups do not necessarily make these contributions, but this list of potential benefits will guide our Audit inquiry.

GIVING VOICE TO CITIZEN INTERESTS

At its most basic, democracy requires periodic free and fair elections in which citizens choose who will govern them. This minimalist understanding of democracy is insufficient, however, to meet the expectations of citizens in a complex modern society. Citizens have a multiplicity of political interests and identities, which they cannot be expected to express in the simple act of periodic voting. For example, imagine an Alberta farmer who is philosophically conservative, favouring low income taxes and limited government. She regularly votes for the Conservative Party, which is elected and re-elected in periodic provincial elections. But the farmer is also deeply concerned about the effects of a sour gas well that is proposed in her area, and believes that the provincial government's regulation of energy companies is inadequate. For our farmer, the tool of periodic elections is an inadequate means of expressing her view and trying to influence the outcome of a decision-making process. She needs to participate immediately, not to wait several years for the next election. She also needs to express her views on this one issue without abandoning the other aspects of her political identity as a fiscal conservative. In short, our farmer needs the option of working through an advocacy group.

This is the first way in which advocacy groups are theoretically important to a modern democratic society: they allow citizens to express the multiplicity of their political interests and identities without having to simplify them or choose among them to make a decision about whom to elect. Thinking back to the roots of democracy in ancient Athens, all citizens (admittedly a narrow segment of Athenian society) could participate directly in all political decisions. Citizens with particular interests thus had the opportunity to make their case directly and participate in the debate. In a representative democracy like Canada's, only an infinitesimally small proportion of the population sits in the legislature and makes decisions. Citizens with an interest in those decisions need some way of making their voices heard before the decision is taken.

Advocacy groups also play a particularly significant role in providing a voice for those interests that are not well represented in mainstream political institutions. One of the first, and most influential, accounts of the place of organized groups in democracies is in the *Federalist Papers* penned by American founding father James Madison. Madison argued that the mobilization of groups, or in his terminology, factions, could counteract the potentially negative aspects of majority rule. In the contemporary era, we often look to advocacy groups to provide a voice for minorities, a category that encompasses both minority opinion and minority groups defined by ascriptive characteristics.

The studies in this series examining legislatures (Docherty 2004), executives (White 2005), and political parties (Cross 2004) document some of the representational failures of these institutions. Advocacy groups have the potential to compensate for such representational failures, particularly with regard to groups that are, or have been, subject to discrimination. While women, Aboriginals, people with disabilities, ethnic minorities, and sexual minorities are underrepresented in Canadian legislatures, organizations exist that seek to speak on their behalf and represent their interests in the policy process. These organizations should not be seen as a substitute for achieving proportionate representation for these groups, but rather as a temporary mechanism counterbalancing representational failures elsewhere in the system.

Providing a Route through Which Citizens Can Participate

Democracy flourishes only when citizens are actively involved in political life. At a minimum, this involves voting in periodic elections. Beyond this minimum requirement, however, we know that democracies fulfill their potential when citizens have the opportunity to involve themselves more extensively in democratic life (Almond and Verba 1963). Democracy is most vibrant when citizens enjoy the freedom to converse about politics, to participate in political activities, and to engage in democratic dialogues with other citizens. When citizens do not avail themselves of these opportunities, their knowledge of and support for the democratic system is less, and political outcomes may well be less responsive to the views of citizens than they would be in a participatory system.

Participation can take a number of forms, including joining a political party, attending a community association meeting, or contacting a government official. From some perspectives, Canadian politics is currently beset by a crisis of nonparticipation. As Gidengil et al. (2004) demonstrate in their volume in this series, voter turnout is in decline, and citizens – especially young Canadians – profess a lack of interest in and knowledge about politics. At least in theory, advocacy groups can serve as a vehicle for citizens' participation. In fact, for Canadians and citizens of other industrialized democracies, participation in democratic life is increasingly channelled through advocacy groups either in addition to or in place of other forms of political activity. Many citizens see advocacy groups as the most effective means for achieving political change, and as a consequence are more likely to engage in group activism than join a political party. While there is some debate as to whether this preference for groups over parties is deleterious for democracy, the fact remains that groups are able to mobilize citizens into periodic participation in the democratic system. To the extent that this is the case, groups contribute to the life of democracy.

FOSTERING DEMOCRATIC CULTURE

Democracy cannot flourish if it is not supported by a democratic culture (Almond and Verba 1963). Democratic culture encompasses both an acceptance of the basic precepts of democracy (equal citizen participation, acceptance of decisions made in a democratic fashion, and general agreement on the basic notion of democratic, or majoritarian, decision making) and a political culture that values and encourages democratic participation. There is substantial evidence that democratic cultures are strengthened when civil society – the space between the purely private realm of the home and the purely public realm of government – is rich in associations that conduct their internal affairs in a democratic and participatory fashion (Putnam 1993). In these associations citizens learn to trust one another, and practise democracy on a small scale, such as by electing a board of directors for their musical group or making decisions governing the operation of a charitable organization by majority vote of members. At least in theory, citizens then transfer their positive attitudes toward democracy and their more nuanced understandings of democracy into the broader political arena, thereby strengthening the societal support for democracy.

Civil society encompasses not only apolitical musical groups and sporting associations but also politicized citizens' groups that advocate various public policies. When these organizations conduct themselves in a democratic fashion in their internal affairs, they can contribute to development and maintenance of a rich civil society. Moreover, to at least the same extent as apolitical civil society organizations, advocacy groups must often wrestle with the more complex problems of democracy. Under what conditions must majority rule be tempered? How can the interests of different demographic groups, like anglophones and francophones or women and men, be accommodated within one organization? How are different views within the group solicited and debated, and how are group positions reached? Under what conditions is a majority inadequate and a consensus required? Thus groups can contribute to the development of a democratic culture that supports a flourishing democracy.

Facilitating the Development of Better Public Policy

One of the resources many advocacy groups have at their disposal is information. Information can be anything from an industry association's detailed knowledge of export markets to an antipoverty group's understanding of how recipients of social services interact with the state. Such information may be based on careful research or more simply on day-to-day experience. For example, one antipoverty group might provide government with detailed studies of poverty rates and causes of poverty, while another might bring an issue to life for decision makers by detailing its members' experiences with hunger or homelessness. In either case, such expertise can potentially assist governments in making good public policy.

Moreover, some political theorists and observers argue that advocacy groups make significant contributions to the quality of democratic deliberation. Mansbridge (1992, 53) contends that groups contribute to deliberative processes in democracy by providing "much of the information and insight that changes the preferences of the public and their elected representatives. They also provide the institutions through which another set of representatives, the interest group elites, deliberates and decides upon the best interests of their constituents and of the polity as a whole." If we accept that deliberation contributes to the quality of public policy, then this deliberative function of advocacy groups is potentially important.

MAKING GOVERNMENT MORE RESPONSIVE TO CITIZENS

Finally, advocacy groups can potentially make governments more responsive to citizens by informing them of the views of segments of the population affected by a policy. For example, a provincial physicians' association can tell governments that its members are strongly opposed to changes in how health care is delivered, and can explain the reasons for this opposition. This does not mean that democracy is best served when governments are slaves to the wishes of certain groups; rather, we expect governments to mediate among competing claims. And governments can perform their mediating function adequately only if they are aware of the perspective of *all* the potentially affected groups – in this example, that would include regional health authorities, patients, and other medical professionals. For this reason, the advocacy group system must be both inclusive and reasonably equitable.

Critiques of Advocacy Groups

The discussion above outlined the ways in which advocacy groups can – at least in theory – contribute to democracy. If this were the only perspective on groups' relationship to democracy, then our task as auditors would be relatively straightforward: to determine the extent to which groups provide a voice for citizens, the extent to which citizens participate in groups, the extent to which groups are internally democratic, the extent to which groups provide information to government, and the extent to which governments are responsive to citizens' concerns.

But this is not the only perspective on groups and democracy. In fact, the terms "interest group," "special interest," and "pressure group" have all become pejorative. This negative perspective is based on the assertion that groups pursuing the interests of relatively limited segments of society will achieve their objectives at the expense of that society's collective good. The most elegant statements of this view stem from rational choice theorist Mancur Olson (1965), who argued that the logic of collective action means that groups with specific economic interests will defeat groups representing the general public. The eventual result of this situation is inefficient governmental regulation, subsidies, and oligarchic economic organization. Others, including Lowi (1979) and Cairns (1985), have argued that the successes of special interests in achieving government programs and subsidies has the effect of restricting governments' ability to cut programs, change direction, and introduce innovative public policy.

The critique of advocacy groups as "special interests" creates strange allies. The first critical argument holds that the groups that mobilize the most consistently and effectively are those that represent elite segments of society. As a consequence, interest mobilization is likely to defend the interests of the affluent and powerful against the interests of the common citizen: Schattschneider's "upper-class accent" of the "pluralist choir." This argument suggests that we must examine carefully which segments of society are mobilized by groups to determine whether societal elites are, in fact, the primary beneficiaries of group action. In addition, we must try to determine which interests are "organized in" to policy discussion by advocacy groups, and which are left out, with particular attention to the question of whether selective economic interests consistently prevail. Finally, we must examine carefully the framework of rules governing the formation, funding, and operation of advocacy groups to determine whether social biases are entrenched in the fundamental rules of the game.

The second critical argument, which has been particularly prominent in recent discussion of groups in Canada, holds that women, minorities, and beneficiaries of government programs are "special" interests that exert undue influence over policy outcomes, taking away from the common good as determined through democratic institutions. This argument conflicts directly with the argument that advocacy groups are particularly important in compensating for the representational failures of other democratic institutions. Our Audit weighs the merits of these two arguments (see Chapters 3 and 5), paying particular attention to the question of whether these compensatory groups are in fact competing with institutions of representative government.

At the heart of modern democracy lie representative institutions that gain their mandates through popular election. The location of popular sovereignty in these institutions is the hallmark of modern democracy. Allegations that advocacy groups compete with, and thereby weaken, representative institutions must consequently be taken seriously. The argument that groups detract from representative democracy is also two-pronged. It suggests, first, that groups compete with political parties as intermediaries between society and the state.

This charge is considered particularly grave because this view also characterizes political parties as capable of mediating among competing interests while groups lack this capacity. Moreover, parties are necessary to structure parliamentary democracy while groups serve no analogous function. From this perspective, to the extent that groups come to replace parties, Canadian democracy loses a capacity for mediation among competing interests as well as a capacity for governance.

The second prong of the argument holds that since the entrenchment of the Canadian Charter of Rights and Freedoms, groups have used the courts to pursue their policy aims and, in so doing, have subverted the central policy-making authority of Parliament. In this view, advocacy groups' use of and preference for litigation as a means of achieving policy change allow unelected judges to replace elected representatives as legislators (Morton and Knopff 2000).

Taken together, these two allegations offer a powerful critique of the contribution of advocacy groups and social movements to Canadian democracy. If they prove founded, these allegations counteract the democratic benefit groups offer in representing citizens in the Canadian polity. Although the task of evaluating the empirical validity of these assertions is difficult, we will examine in some detail the relationship between political parties and interest groups (see Chapter 3) and interest groups' use of the courts in Canada (see Chapter 7) in an effort to measure the weight of these claims.

A third set of critiques of advocacy groups as democratic actors focuses on the quality of participation groups offer. According to this argument, group participation brings out citizens' basest instinct: to pursue their own self-interest over the common good, and to do so in a rigid and uncompromising manner. Critics of advocacy groups assert that the single-issue focus of some groups makes them lose sight of the bigger picture. Environmental groups, in this view, may demand emission controls without taking into account their impact on the economy, or groups representing people in need of a particular medical treatment may not consider the effect of this action on the government's ability to provide other services (see, for example, Stanbury 2000). A single-minded focus may make groups unwilling to compromise on the issues they consider to be important, even when such compromise would be in the public interest.

Moreover, group leaders have an incentive to exaggerate their claims, prolong conflicts, and engage in publicity stunts in an effort to raise money from supporters. High-profile activities like blockading a logging road to protest logging in old-growth forest or putting pigs on the lawn of the Parliament buildings to shame politicians accepting government pensions get publicity for groups, and publicity helps raise money. But critics of advocacy groups point out that these kinds of activities contribute little to discussions of public policy and may make it more difficult for governments to find compromises among competing interests.

From an Audit perspective, the relevant question is not whether groups and their members are uncompromising, but rather whether the mechanisms in place for governments to consult with groups lend themselves to negotiation and conciliation, rather than unresolved conflict. With this consideration in mind, Chapters 6 and 7 examine the range of mechanisms in place for governments to interact with advocacy groups and evaluate whether these mechanisms promote compromise.

Evaluating the Evidence

This review of theoretical perspectives on the role of advocacy groups in modern democracies shows that our audit must not only evaluate the extent to which advocacy groups are able to live up to theoretical expectations that they give voice to citizens' interests, provide a route through which citizens can participate, support democratic culture, facilitate the development of good public policy, and make government more responsive to citizens. In addition to this, we must give careful consideration to arguments that advocacy groups detract from democracy. It is essential to evaluate the claim that advocacy group mobilization favours business and the wealthy, as well as the claim that "special" interests are able to prevail over the common interest. We must also examine the interplay between advocacy groups and representative institutions with a view to determining whether advocacy groups in fact contribute to a decline in these institutions. With these objectives in mind, we now turn to our findings.

WHO PARTICIPATES
IN ADVOCACY GROUPS?

3

Advocacy groups potentially offer a vehicle for citizens to participate in the democratic process. Our first task as auditors is to measure the extent to which this is the case: how many citizens belong to advocacy groups? We must also address the question of equality of participation: which citizens are more inclined to be active in these groups, and what effect does this participation have on activists' political beliefs and other political activities? The Audit values at stake in this discussion are participation and inclusiveness.

When we think about participation in advocacy groups, our first consideration is not only the amount of citizen participation that is channelled through these groups, but also the quality of that participation. Are advocacy group members deeply involved in these organizations, or do they simply send money to the group as a signal of their support? If advocacy groups are to expand the opportunities for citizens to participate in Canadian democracy, members should be actively involved in the internal operations of their groups. Merely holding a membership in a group is the most minimal form of political participation. For this reason we must closely examine not just the number of people who are involved in these groups, but also the extent and the quality of their involvement.

There is another crucial dimension to our examination of participation: does participation in advocacy groups improve or detract from the quality of democratic citizenship in Canada? Many political scientists argue that mass involvement in voluntary associations is an important condition for a stable political democracy and that these organizations of civil society help to train people politically. Participation exposes members to political cues and messages, enables them to develop organizational and communication skills that are easily transferable to politics, and provides opportunities for recruitment to other political activities (see Almond and Verba 1963; Olsen 1972; Verba, Schlozman, and Brady 1995, 40). More recently, Robert Putnam (2000) and others have argued that involvement in voluntary organizations contributes to social trust, cooperativeness, and support for the norms of democracy. This chapter assesses the degree to which participation in advocacy groups enhances political trust, confidence in government, and commitment to democratic values.

Not all observers anticipate that involvement in advocacy groups will have entirely salutary effects. Critics claim that groups may detract from democracy by encouraging citizens to bypass traditional democratic processes such as voting, involvement in political parties, and contacting elected officials in favour of less traditional tactics such as street protests, boycotts, and civil disobedience. In this view, these more confrontational tactics debase the formal political process and make it more difficult to reach compromises on policy questions. We therefore examine the relationship between membership in interest groups and engagement in various conventional and unconventional forms of political activity.

The inclusiveness of the Canadian political system is also at stake in this chapter. Theoretical accounts of advocacy group involvement in contemporary democracies produce two very different sets of expectations about which segments of Canadian society will join these groups. Critical accounts suggest that individuals with greater wealth and social status will be overrepresented among group members, reflecting patterns of inequality and exclusion in the society at large. A competing view suggests that the mobilization of citizen-based, equality-seeking groups and social movements in recent decades means that advocacy groups help to inject a wider range of voices into political debates. In particular, the mobilization of social movements of women, environmentalists, and a number of minority groups predicts that participation in advocacy groups should be more socially inclusive than participation in traditional organizations. To assess these two competing sets of expectations, we examine the backgrounds and characteristics of individuals who are members of advocacy groups, and we compare them to members of more traditional organizations – political parties.

Mapping Group Members

How many Canadians participate in advocacy groups? This question is best answered by looking at large public opinion surveys such as the Canadian Election Studies (CES) or the World Values Surveys that ask respondents about their involvement in groups. Using survey data of this kind, especially when the survey questions were designed with a somewhat different research purpose in mind is, of course, less satisfying than developing questions for our particular purposes. Undertaking such research went beyond the scope and resources of this project, however, so we are forced to rely on secondary analysis of data. Despite the limitations of such analysis, we believe that this is the only feasible way to estimate rates, patterns, and behavioural consequences of group membership among Canadians in a systematic way.

Although the question "How many Canadians belong, or have in the past belonged, to advocacy groups?" appears deceptively simple, the answer naturally depends on how one defines advocacy groups. The CES used the term "interest groups." The 2000 Canadian Election Study asked, "Have you ever been a member of an interest group that worked for change on a particular social or political issue?" The approximately 11 percent of adult citizens who answered yes constitute the rate of group membership using a narrow definition – a group that is dedicated to working for change on a particular issue. To reflect the question wording employed here, we will refer to groups as "interest groups" in the segments of this chapter that use the CES data.

As noted in Chapter 1, however, many organizations that do not have as their first purpose influence of public policy, including unions, professional associations, and religious organizations, do on occasion act like interest groups. These groups would probably not have come to mind when survey respondents answered the question about interest group membership. Using a broader definition of advocacy group, participation rates are much higher: according to the 2000 CES, 10 percent claimed current or past membership in a voluntary organization, 18 percent in a labour union, and 25 percent in a professional association.

Over the past twenty-five years the proportion of Canadians who belong to women's groups, environmental groups, labour unions, professional associations, and voluntary organizations linked to community service, social welfare, and health has increased. As we see in Table 3.1, in 1981 only a quarter of Canadians were involved in these types of associations. By 2000 almost four in ten survey respondents

Table 3.1

Canadian involvement in interest-group-like organizations

	1981 (%)	1990 (%)	2000 (%)
Women's groups	n/a	7	10
Environmental groups	5	8	8
Labour unions	11	12	13
Professional organizations	12	16	16
Voluntary groups: community service/social welfare/health	13	17	24
Total population involved in interest-group-like organizations	24	34	39

Source: World Values Surveys 1981-2000.

indicated that they were members of such groups. While the figures resulting from the narrow definition of interest group activism probably underestimate the full extent of participation in groups, the figures resulting from the broader definition similarly overestimate the extent of participation. Membership in some unions and professional associations is mandatory and may not reflect an individual's decision to join. Nonetheless, through newsletters or other forms of communication these organizations provide even their passive members with important information about their group's interactions with governments and may increase their awareness of political issues of relevance to them.

Are Canadians as active in groups and associations as citizens of other Western industrialized democracies? The answer to this question is a resounding yes. As Table 3.2 shows, more Canadians indicate that they are involved in interest-group-like associations than citizens of Britain, France, or Germany. Only Americans are more active than Canadians in such organizations, a finding that is supported by past research on voluntary associations (Curtis, Grabb, and Baer 1992; Dekker and van den Broek 1998). It is particularly interesting to note that rates of participation are increasing in Canada and the United States while they are declining in the three European cases included in this comparison. This is due in part to declines in union memberships in Europe, particularly in France and Britain, and a notable increase in involvement in women's groups, environmental organizations, and voluntary organizations linked to community service, social welfare, and health in Canada and the United States.

How do rates of participation in advocacy groups compare to involvement in political parties, which are a more traditional vehicle

Table 3.2

Cross-national involvement in various interest-group-like organizations

	1981 (%)	1990 (%)	2000 (%)
Canada	24.4	34.1	39.2
Britain	29.8	29.2	12.4
France	13.0	12.8	10.6
West Germany	25.1	30.7	16.5
United States	26.5	32.6	54.3

Note: These figures are derived by adding the rates of reported participation in the five categories of organization listed in Table 3.1.
Source: World Values Surveys 1981-2000.

for political involvement? Just over one-tenth of the respondents to the 2000 Canadian Election Study claimed to have been members of interest groups at some time (using our narrow definition), while almost twice as many respondents (19 percent) claimed to have belonged to a political party. Of course, a person may be involved in both a group and a party, as 4 percent of the respondents were. On the other hand, 74 percent claimed never to have been involved in either a formal interest group or a political party. These numbers indicate that while interest group membership is growing, it has not overtaken party membership, and indeed a particularly activist segment of the population combines involvement in an interest group with partisan political involvement.

Overall, then, we find that participation in advocacy groups is relatively robust. It lags behind participation in political parties, but it compares favourably to rates of participation in other industrialized democracies. Moreover, the general trend is toward greater participation over time.

Who Participates?

Who are the people who increasingly participate in these groups? Very few studies explore the background of interest group activists in Canada. One study, however, examined individual participation in an Alberta environmental interest group (Archer and Alford 1997). The study found little to support the idea that groups were more inclusive than other institutions. Members of the Alberta Wilderness Association did not resemble the Alberta population but tended to be middle-aged, higher income, and well-educated males. Studies of associational memberships in other countries have yielded similar results (Moyser and Parry 1997).

Likewise, studies have found that a majority of party members – the traditional route for citizen participation – tend to be white males of higher socioeconomic status than the general population (see Cross 2004). If interest groups were indeed playing a compensatory role, we would expect that their members would be younger, less well educated, less wealthy, and more likely to be female or of a minority background than party members. Comparing the two groups allows us to determine whether interest groups are in fact more inclusive than traditional political organizations. For the purposes of this comparison, we use the narrow definition of interest group membership, as this more accurately captures those individuals who have chosen to join an organization devoted to advocacy activities.

Table 3.3 presents the differences in the percentage of various groups in society that have been actively involved in traditional political institutions and those involved in interest groups. These data tell us that interest group membership is, in fact, more common among those with higher social status: people with jobs, white skin, university educations, and higher family incomes. We think it is particularly important to note the strong impact that postsecondary education and income have on rates of participation: this demonstrates that citizens with the cognitive and material resources that education brings are more inclined toward participation in advocacy groups. This echoes the findings in Gidengil et al. (2004) in this series.

Even though interest group membership reflects patterns of inequality in society as a whole, interest groups are nonetheless more inclusive of diversity in their membership than are political parties. As shown in Table 3.3, interest group activists differ from party members in Canada in four ways. First, women remain slightly less likely than men to have been members of a political party. The pattern shown in Table 3.3 reflects similar findings in studies of political party members (Young and Cross 2003). However, the gender differences among interest group activists are not statistically significant, which means that while present in the survey they are not likely to be found within the broader population. Although the differences between the two kinds of members are small, they suggest that interest group membership is slightly more inclusive of women than party membership. The near-equality of gender among advocacy group members probably reflects the fact that many interest groups have mobilized around questions of

Table 3.3

Participation in interest groups and political parties by different social groups

		Interest group members (%)	Party members (%)
Gender	Women	9.7	16.9
	Men	11.4	20.1
	Difference	−1.7	−3.2*
Employment	Unemployed	8.0	13.6
	Employed	11.5	18.3
	Difference	−3.5	−4.7**
Ethnicity	Minority	4.1	11.6
	Non-minority	11.0	18.9
	Difference	−6.9**	−7.3*
Income	Under $30,000	8.9	17.0
	$30,000-60,000	9.3	19.8
	Over $60,000	13.5	19.9
	Difference	−4.2**	−2.9
Education	High school	6.8	16.2
	University	18.9	23.8
	Difference	−12.1**	−7.6**
Age (birth year)	post-1971	6.5	4.8
	1961-70	9.5	15.1
	1946-60	12.3	21.5
	pre-1945	12.6	27.5

* p < .05
** p < .01
Source: Canadian Election Study 2000.

equality; in particular, many women's groups have been established to pressure governments on issues such as employment equity, access to abortion, or protection from violence.

While interest groups appear to be slightly more inclusive of women, they appear to be less inclusive of low-income Canadians. Individuals with family incomes over $60,000 dominate interest group membership to a greater extent than they do political party membership. While political parties clearly provide some barriers to individuals with lower financial resources, the differences in the participation rates of lower- and higher-income individuals is in fact not statistically significant. We suspect that these differences are at least partly a function of the ways advocacy groups in Canada organize. Chapter 4 discusses the growing trend toward advocacy groups that encourage only "chequebook participation" from their members; these groups are more interested in soliciting donations than volunteers. This trend makes advocacy group membership much more available to Canadians who have higher disposable incomes.

Third, university education is a stronger determinant of participation in an interest group than a political party. Almost 19 percent of respondents with a university education indicated that they had been involved in an interest group, while only 7 percent of those without a university education had done so. While more educated Canadians are also more likely to be involved in political parties than those with lower levels of education, the difference in their involvement is larger among interest group activists. Interest groups appear to be the chosen vehicle of those with higher levels of education. This finding is consistent with arguments that well-educated citizens possess the political skills and resources necessary to be interested and involved in politics, but are less reliant on traditional political authorities such as parties to provide the cues to guide their involvement (Dalton 1988; Nevitte 1996).

The only segment of the population that is more represented in interest groups than in political parties is youth. As Table 3.3 shows, more Canadians aged thirty and under indicated they are involved in an interest group than in a political party. This finding should not be misinterpreted: the difference appears because young Canadians are particularly uninvolved in parties. Canadians under the age of thirty are still *less* likely than older Canadians to be involved in an interest group. This lower rate of participation is part of a larger phenomenon of young Canadians tuning out of political life entirely, and as such is a reason for great concern. This trend is discussed in detail in Gidengil et al. (2004).

Table 3.3 also shows that ethnic minorities and unemployed Canadians are underrepresented to a similar degree in both political parties and interest groups. These are both segments of Canadian society particularly at risk for social marginalization. Unlike the case of women, whose mobilization into women's groups has apparently offset patterns of underrepresentation that would otherwise have been found, the mobilization of ethnic minorities into lobby organizations has apparently not been sufficient to offset patterns of underrepresentation in interest groups more broadly.

In general, these results seem to discount the argument that interest groups mobilize different segments of Canadian society to be-

Table 3.4

Social cleavages and participatory differences in various groups

	Community service (%)	Professional associations (%)	Labour union (%)	Environmental group (%)	Women's group (%)
Gender (female/male)	6.8**	−2.2	−7.1	−1.7	n/a
Education (no university/ university education)	−11.8**	−28.9**	9.6	−3.3*	−3.4*
Ethnicity (minority/non-minority)	−2.3	2.2	−18.6	−1.0	3.3
Employment (unemployed/employed)	−4.5**	−12.5**	−4.5	1.6	5.6**
Income (<$30,000/>$60,000)	−2.2	−24.3**	−9.4	−0.2	2.6

Note: The values represent the percentage point difference between the paired groups being compared in each case.
* $p < .05$
** $p < .01$
Source: Canadian Election Study 2000.

come involved in politics than do more traditional institutions such as political parties. Low-income Canadians, the unemployed, the poorly educated, and ethnic minorities are no more inclined to participate in interest groups than in political parties. That said, a more nuanced picture appears when we look more closely at the backgrounds of members in specific types of groups. Table 3.4 reveals that community service groups, professional associations, and labour unions all tend to have members that are disproportionately well educated, higher income, and from majority ethnic groups. However, environmental groups and women's groups, which have emerged over the last four decades, offer more participatory opportunities for traditionally excluded citizens. In these organizations, differences in involvement rates of people coming from different socioeconomic backgrounds are small and generally not statistically significant.

These data suggest that an audit of the degree of inclusiveness of Canadian interest groups must take into account the nature of the different types of groups. While traditional organizations such as community service groups, professional associations, and labour unions are slightly more accessible to those who have long been excluded from parties, they still tend to be dominated by older, white, well-educated individuals. Organizations such as environmental or women's groups clearly function under different guiding principles. Emerging as part of a social movement mobilization in the 1960s and 1970s, these types of groups are generally structured to enhance inclusion. As a result, they tend to be more accessible to and may even seek out members from a wide range of backgrounds. Thus, we can conclude that while in general interest group activists tend to be drawn from social and economic elites, some organizations, such as environmental and women's groups, play an important role in addressing the representational deficits of traditional political institutions.

The Quality of Participation

The next question we must address in our audit of the participatory aspect of advocacy groups is whether these organizations allow for active participation by their members. Participation in advocacy groups may range from simply purchasing a membership to taking on leadership roles within the organization. While John Stuart Mill ([1861] 1972, 217) wrote that "any participation, even in the smallest public function is useful," from an Audit perspective we would argue that active participation in the day-to-day activities of a group is of greater benefit to Canadian democracy than passive membership. Active participation engages citizens in the democratic process, brings them in contact with other citizens, and forces them to confront the dilemmas of process and accommodation that inevitably accompany group activity.

Comparative studies have found that the extent of citizen involvement in groups and other voluntary associations varies from country to country (Dekker and van den Broek 1998). European countries tend to have either high levels of group membership or high rates of membership participation, but seldom both. Canada and the United States are unique in that they are "activist" civil societies that possess widespread group membership *and* high levels of voluntary activity among these members.

Although little work has examined the degree to which Canadians are active in interest groups, a public opinion survey conducted in 2000 by the Institute for Research in Public Policy found that 89 percent of the people who had belonged to an interest group indicated that they had attended group meetings or had volunteered time on behalf of the group (Howe and Northrup 2000). Archer and Alford's (1997) study focusing specifically on the Alberta Wilderness Association found that members regularly read the organization's newsletter (89 percent), gave money to the organization (57 percent), voted for the board of directors (56 percent), and wrote letters to the government on behalf of the organization (44 percent). However, only 22 percent volunteered up to five hours per month for the organization and less than 10 percent attended the annual general meeting or actually served on the board (146-7). In this respect, interest group members are much less active than members of political parties. In their study of political party members, Cross and Young found that 46 percent of party members spent between one and five hours on party activity in an average month, and over 60 percent had attended at least one party meeting in the prior year (see Cross 2004, ch. 2).

This limited evidence shows that Canadians who claim to be members of interest groups also claim to be active in these organizations. Our data do not allow us to determine which types of organizations citizens are the most active in, but the results of other studies suggest that that the nature of the organization affects the extent of activism. For example, caring organizations, educational or self-help organizations, and community-oriented organizations attract a small but relatively active membership (Dekker and van den Broek 1996, 133; Moyser and Parry 1997, 29). Those groups with the highest percentage of inactive members were political associations or occupationally based organizations (members of unions, staff organizations, or professional associations). This research also found that the groups with the most active memberships also appeared to share leadership responsibilities among a wider number of members than those with more limited membership involvement. Comparable research needs to be conducted in Canada.

These findings raise a number of questions about how Canadian advocacy groups organize themselves. Extensive and meaningful participation can occur only when groups are organized in a manner that permits, or even encourages, it. Chapter 4 examines these issues in greater detail, focusing on the roles and entitlements of members in Canadian advocacy groups.

Democratic Culture

One of the most important debates surrounding advocacy groups centres on whether the activism they foster contributes to or detracts from democracy. Supporters of groups see many benefits in associational involvement. Putnam (2000) argues that being part of a group or community organization brings people into contact with others who do not always share the same backgrounds or values. This interaction, which "bridges" different social groups, enhances social trust among citizens and establishes norms of reciprocity that create what he refers to as "social capital." In turn, this social capital leads to a more politically active citizenry, better education and health care, economic prosperity, and a reduction in crime. It should be noted that Putnam is writing specifically about organizations, many of them apolitical, whose membership base spans salient social cleavages. This assumption does not always hold true for advocacy groups.

In fact, some critics claim that some advocacy groups are more likely to exert negative rather than positive impacts on society. Groups may attract people with similar points of view or experiences: some advocacy groups construct their membership very narrowly to include only individuals who share a salient characteristic like a religious affiliation, ethnic heritage, or sexual orientation. These sorts of groups have been referred to as "bonding groups," because they bond people together and reinforce shared perspectives. As a result, prejudice and distrust of others is continually reinforced through contact with like-minded individuals (Maloney, Smith, and Stoker 2000, 218). The classic example that is regularly raised to demonstrate this point is the Ku Klux Klan, whose members reinforce each others' extremist points of view. Furthermore, this self-reinforcement may lead to feelings of alienation when governments do not respond to the concerns of group members, who believe that their views are widely shared. Of course, even within groups that share one salient characteristic there are likely to be other cleavages that require some effort toward accommodation.

Questions relating to the quality of participation are of particular concern for so-called chequebook groups. In these mass-membership organizations, such as Greenpeace and the Canadian Taxpayers Federation, the relationship between members and the group is often purely financial (Maloney and Jordan 1997; Stanbury 2000). They are run by paid staff and provide their members with limited opportunities for participation. In most cases members have been recruited through marketing techniques and are encouraged to feel alienated from the political system and more intolerant of opposing views by the nature of the information they are sent through direct mail (Maloney 1999, 112; Stanbury 2000). For example, in his comparison of organizational members recruited through social networks and direct marketing Goodwin (1988) found that direct mail joiners were of two types. They were either already very committed to a cause and easily mobilized, or they had relatively low levels of commitment and interest and were persuaded to join only as a result of the direct mail solicitations. Members recruited through social networks fell between these two extremes, showing concern and commitment for the issue, but not to the extreme that some of the direct mail members did. Furthermore, the direct mail recruits consistently scored higher than those recruited through social networks in terms of extremist views on an issue, intolerance for other points of view, and political alienation. This may be because the information that groups use to recruit and maintain members in their direct mail solicitations emphasizes aspects of a problem that may arouse anxiety, anger, or fear (Stanbury 2000, 315). Goodwin's only positive result was that levels of alienation and aggression on an issue declined the longer individuals remained members of chequebook organizations (1988, 64).

While some groups do mobilize their members around very narrow issues and may reinforce views that isolate them from alternative perspectives, most research has shown that involvement in voluntary associations is positively related to trust in others (Dekker and van den Broek 1996, 138; Putnam 2000, 137). This is certainly the case in Canada, where individuals who claim to be members of an interest group demonstrate higher levels of trust for others than citizens do who do not report membership in an interest group. According to 2000 Canadian Election Study data, almost 70 percent of those who are involved in interest groups believe that most people can be trusted, as compared to 55 percent of those who are not involved in interest groups. In fact, the level of generalized trust was higher among interest group members than among members of political parties (62 percent).

Another positive outcome of group involvement relates to the political socialization role played by groups. In arguing that civic involvement is a factor explaining political participation, Verba, Schlozman, and Brady (1995, 40) note that there are three ways that activity in groups has a politicizing effect. First, this involvement leads to the development of organizational and communication skills that are easily transferred to politics. Second, such involvement may result in opportunities for recruitment to more formal political activities. And, third, involvement in groups may provide exposure to political messages and cues that may stimulate interest in and awareness of politics. They conclude by arguing that organizational involvement matters to political participation because it provides training in the civic skills that are important for political engagement (336). For this reason institutions of civil society such as interest groups and voluntary associations have been called "schools of democracy" (Tocqueville [1831] 1969).

Results similar to those in the United States (Verba, Schlozman, and Brady 1995) are found in Canada as well. Data from the 2000 Canadian

Election Study reveal that members of interest groups are much more interested in what is happening on the political scene than are those who belong to neither parties nor groups, and demonstrate the same levels of interest in politics as do members of political parties. On a scale of zero to ten, where zero means not very interested and ten means very interested, interest group members score an average of 6.7. Party members average 6.6 and non-interest group members average 5.8 on the scale.

As Table 3.5 indicates, when it comes to various other forms of conventional political participation, interest group activists demonstrate high levels of political activity. Contrary to suggestions that involvement in interest groups detracts from traditional forms of participation, interest group members are much more likely than nonmembers to engage with the institutions of representative government and to be involved in electoral politics. Group members are far more likely to have contacted an elected representative than nonmembers, and are even 17 percentage points more likely to write, call, or e-mail their MP than are members of political parties.

At election time, interest group members turn out to vote at the same rate as party members and, again, are much more likely to vote than those who are not involved in interest groups. Because nonvoters are also less likely to answer surveys, surveys do tend to overreport turnout rates, and in fact turnout in the 2000 federal election was much lower than the rates suggested in Table 3.5. There is, however, no reason to believe that this bias in the sample is disproportionately found among group members or nonmembers, so we can compare groups with a reasonable degree of certainty. Remarkably, interest group members are even more likely to volunteer in election campaigns

Table 3.5

Political participation rates for interest group and party members

	Interest group members (%)	Non-group members (%)	Party members (%)
Contacted MP	73.6	29.2	56.5
Voted in 2000 election	92.2	81.7	91.4
Worked for party during campaign	19.2	7.5	18.3
Discuss politics often	47.1	22.6	39.0

Source: Canadian Election Study 2000.

Who Participates in Advocacy Groups?

than are party members. Group members are also more likely to talk about elections than party members and are far more likely to do so than non-group members. In short, of the three groupings included in Table 3.5, interest group members are by far the most active and involved democratic citizens.

In looking at this data it is important to note that Verba and Nie (1972, 182) found that while members of organizations are more likely to be active in political life than are nonmembers, increased political participation was linked only to active membership: "The individual who is a *passive* member in one or more organizations is *no more likely* to be active in politics than the individual who belongs to no such association. In contrast, the active organizational member is much more likely than the non-member to be politically active" (186, italics in original). More recent studies support the strong link between active involvement in voluntary associations and higher levels of political involvement, but also find that inactive joiners, while less politically involved, still have higher-than-average levels of political interest and sense of competence (Moyser and Parry 1997, 41; Dekker and van den Broek 1996, 138).

Table 3.6 lists such unconventional forms of political participation as signing a petition, boycotting a business, attending a lawful demonstration, participating in an illegal strike, and occupying a building. These activities are often associated with interest groups, but it is not just interest group activists who support these types of behaviours. As Table 3.6 indicates, interest group members were more likely than nonmembers to claim to have signed petitions, boycotted products, and attended lawful demonstrations, but differences in their *willingness* to consider these types of activities is slight. Over 98 percent of Canadians (whether group members or not) have already signed, or would be willing to sign, a petition; almost 85 percent have already participated, or would be prepared to participate, in a product boycott or lawful demonstration. These results contradict arguments portraying interest group activists as alienated from the political system and turned off of the democratic process. Indeed, there can be little argument that memberships in interest groups enhance democratic participation. If turning out to vote during elections, working on campaigns, and communicating with governments through petitions, protests, and demonstrations are all important forms of political participation, then interest group members are certainly politically active.

But can it be argued that group members are also active in negative ways? Do they engage in activities that are illegal or involve violence

Table 3.6

Participation in unconventional forms of political activity

		Have done (%)	Might do (%)	Would never do (%)
Sign a petition	Interest group members	95.7	3.2	1.1
	Non-group members	84.4	14.2	1.4
	Party members	94.4	5.2	0.3
Boycott a business	Interest group members	48.9	44.9	6.2
	Non-group members	24.7	58.1	17.2
	Party members	42.6	45.1	12.3
Lawful demonstration	Interest group members	47.5	41.2	11.3
	Non-group members	21.0	61.5	17.5
	Party members	38.3	46.7	15.0
Illegal strike	Interest group members	8.7	34.2	57.0
	Non-group members	6.5	26.2	67.3
	Party members	12.4	22.8	64.8
Occupy a building	Interest group members	4.7	21.3	74.0
	Non-group members	2.2	19.0	78.8
	Party members	1.9	19.5	76.5

Source: Canadian Election Study 2000.

and that have the potential to undermine the Canadian state? We would argue no. As Table 3.6 also shows, while interest group members are slightly more willing than nonmembers to consider activities like striking illegally or occupying a building, they are not noticeably more likely to engage in these actions. Less than 9 percent of interest group members have participated in these more extreme forms of political activity, and more party members have participated in an illegal strike than interest group members. We note that the legitimacy of protest tactics is a thorny issue, which we return to in Chapter 7.

There is some debate about the degree to which these unconventional activities are related to active involvement in interest groups. For example, Archer and Alford (1997) found that support for radical action was greatest among the most active members of the Alberta Wilderness Association. This support declined the longer individuals had been involved in the group (153). Dekker and van den Broek (1996) also found that in the United States, Great Britain, and Germany,

Who Participates in Advocacy Groups?

active group members are more likely to support unconventional forms of participation than are passive members. However, some evidence exists that active members are less likely to actually *engage* in these behaviours (Billiet and Cambré 1999).

Despite claims that participation in advocacy groups leads to political polarization, increased cynicism about government's capacity to solve problems, and declining confidence in the effectiveness of civic engagement, our findings demonstrate that citizen involvement in advocacy groups strengthens Canadian democracy. Public opinion studies in Canada and elsewhere indicate that interest group involvement is linked to support of and satisfaction with the democratic system. Data from the 2000 Canadian Election Study show that while the levels of satisfaction with democracy in Canada among interest group members are slightly lower than among non-group members (62 percent of group members indicate they are very or fairly satisfied as compared to 69 percent of nonmembers), the levels are higher than among party members (60 percent). Likewise, levels of confidence in the federal government are similar among group members (47 percent) and non-group members (47 percent), both of which are higher than the levels of confidence exhibited by party members (44 percent). Nothing in these results suggests that interest groups do anything but help to establish and maintain a democratic culture in Canada.

Evaluating Citizen Participation in Advocacy Groups

Citizen participation in advocacy groups has increased in Canada over recent decades, and Canadians are among the most actively involved members of such organizations in the world. After examining competing claims about the benefits and drawbacks of this advocacy group mobilization, we conclude that these groups appear to be slightly more accessible to citizens who have traditionally lacked political representation in other democratic institutions such as parties. However, most groups are still dominated by older, white, and well-educated individuals. While this finding belies claims that groups generally represent "special interests" that differ from those traditionally addressed by parties or Parliament, it underscores the importance of those groups that do attempt to play a compensatory role in the system.

A second conclusion that we have drawn is that participation, and in particular *active* participation, in advocacy groups is strongly linked to the establishment and maintenance of a democratic culture. Group members are politically engaged and demonstrate strong support for the democratic process. While they are slightly more likely to have participated in more unconventional political activities, they demonstrate little support for the use of violence or other possibly illegal methods of getting their messages across. The quality of engagement in group activities is important, and active participation in group activities and decision making should be encouraged. As a result, we are concerned about the growing number of "chequebook" organizations that claim large memberships whose participation is purely financial. While membership in such groups may lead to greater political awareness and involvement, we fear that this participation by proxy may lead to a growing alienation from the political system and a decline in tolerance for alternative points of view. With this in mind, we now turn to an examination of how Canadian advocacy groups organize themselves.

Chapter 3
___

Strengths

- Canada is among those nations whose citizens demonstrate the most involvement in groups.

- Compensatory organizations and groups established as a result of the new social movements of the later twentieth century are open to traditionally underrepresented segments of Canadian society.

- Active involvement in interest groups is positively related to heightened political participation and support for a democratic culture in Canada.

Weaknesses

- While more accessible than other representative institutions, many interest groups are still dominated by older, white, and well-educated Canadians, weakening their ability to compensate for the underrepresentation of some groups in political institutions.

4 THE INTERNAL LIFE OF GROUPS

As argued in Chapter 2, advocacy groups have the potential to make significant contributions to Canadian democracy by providing a vehicle for citizens to participate in public affairs, giving citizens experience with the give and take of democratic life within organizations, and bringing voices into the public sphere that would otherwise be neglected. This argument is premised on several assumptions, two of which are crucial: first, that advocacy groups have the potential to be internally democratic organizations that encourage citizens to participate and, second, that these groups have the capacity to act as authentic representatives of the collectivities on whose behalf they speak. To check the validity of these assumptions, we focus now on the internal life of Canadian advocacy groups. Are groups representative of the diversity of their constituencies? Do they organize themselves democratically? Do they encourage members to participate? Are group leaders accountable to group members? These questions involve all three Audit values of inclusiveness, participation, and responsiveness.

We must acknowledge at the outset how difficult it is to generalize about how well Canadian groups perform in these respects. Even a cursory examination of the internal organization and practices of Canadian groups reveals the tremendous diversity of organizational forms they embrace. Nonetheless, by examining the practices of a wide range of groups as they relate to our three Audit values we can highlight those that most closely approximate the democratic ideal. We will also consider the factors that discourage groups from embracing these best practices, and the measures that might assist groups in moving toward democratic goals.

As noted in Chapter 3, participation in democratic processes within groups has merit in itself, as it gives citizens the experience of democracy, complete with the need to accommodate competing views, accept majority decisions, and find inclusive processes of decision making. But when group members are involved directly in charting their group's policy direction on an issue, there is an additional benefit: the group can then present a policy stance that is an authentic representation of its members' views. This increases the group's legitimacy in the broader policy process and allows it to contribute more decisively to the wider policy debate.

Some groups face higher expectations than do others in regard to democratic inclusiveness, participation, and responsiveness. For instance, organizations representing business are not expected to engage citizens in democratic discussion. Groups established to pursue the interests of an industry may contribute to the public debate by providing relevant information and expressing the views of companies in their sector, but they are not constituted as democratic vehicles. Rather, the burden of our expectations is borne by citizens' groups lobbying on behalf of some collectivity of Canadians, or to achieve policy change in the public interest. Groups that want to represent Canadians who share some characteristic, interest, or opinion have the potential to engage citizens in an internally democratic process. Examples of such groups include the National Action Committee on the Status of Women, Equality for Gays and Lesbians Everywhere (EGALE), the Canadian Taxpayers Federation, and the Council of Canadians, all of which are discussed in some detail in this chapter.

The demands for internal democracy and inclusiveness weigh most heavily on the organizations that we term "compensatory" groups. These are groups that try to speak for collectivities of Canadians who are otherwise not well represented in mainstream political institutions. To the extent that women, members of ethnic minorities, gays and lesbians, the disabled, and others are underrepresented in legislatures, executives, the courts, and political parties, we look to advocacy groups to compensate for this underrepresentation by injecting the concerns of these citizens into public policy discussion. This expectation imposes extraordinarily high standards on these groups – essentially, largely self-financing collections of volunteers are expected to make up for the failures of well-funded, professionalized democratic institutions. But fair or not, groups that purport to speak for underrepresented collectivities bear the additional representational burden of trying to be inclusive of diversity within their constituency, and to be responsive to the interests and opinions of members of that constituency. On account of this special representational expectation, we pay particular attention to these compensatory groups in our analysis of the internal life of groups.

Inclusiveness

In Chapter 3, we reported that advocacy group membership appears to be somewhat more socially inclusive than some other forms of political participation, most notably membership in political parties. That said, young Canadians, visible minorities, and to a lesser extent women tend to be underrepresented among group members. Compounding this, group members tend to be better educated and more affluent than nonmembers. These patterns suggest that income, education, and social status provide individuals with the resources, skills, and confidence that make participation possible. In this chapter, we shift our focus to the other side of the equation: what do groups do to encourage or discourage inclusiveness among their memberships?

The definition of inclusiveness within groups will vary depending on the particular context of the group. National groups struggle with inclusiveness along the lines of language and region, as well as ethnicity and gender. Even groups that are organized according to a shared characteristic must confront issues of inclusiveness: for instance, women's organizations must take into account ethnicity, language, region, sexual orientation, and physical ability. Ironically, the organizations representing politically excluded groups, like women or the disabled, face some of the greatest pressure to be internally inclusive, largely as a result of the ideologies of inclusion that they espouse.

Canadian groups vary considerably in terms of their efforts to be inclusive of social diversity. Many organizations concern themselves little with the issue. For example, the Canadian Council of Chief Executives (formerly the Business Council on National Issues) restricts its membership to the CEOs of the top 150 corporations in the country. A quick glance at the group's membership makes it clear that very few of the organization's members have an ethnic origin other than British or French, and even fewer are women. These patterns reflect the barriers to inclusiveness embedded in Canadian corporate culture.

Other groups structure themselves to achieve inclusiveness along regional or linguistic lines. Regional and linguistic cleavages are highly salient in Canada, and are reinforced by the institutions of federalism. Many national organizations are confederal in their organization, which is to say made up of provincial units. In these cases, regional representation is embedded in the group's fundamental organization, with the national board made up of provincial representatives. For example, the Canadian Automobile Association, an advocacy group for motorists, is comprised of provincial and, in the case of Ontario, five regional member associations that send delegates to the organization's annual meeting (CAA 2003). This structure ensures regional representation on the organization's board. Other groups use informal measures to achieve regional representation. For instance, when electing its board of directors, the Council of Canadians employs a nominating committee that has the task of "recognizing the importance of reflecting Canadian diversity, regional membership and activity" (Council of Canadians 2003).

More traditional advocacy groups like the Canadian Chamber of Commerce or the Consumers' Association of Canada devote little attention to questions of inclusiveness in terms of gender, ethnicity, or other ascriptive characteristics. This does not necessarily mean that they are not internally inclusive, but rather that these dimensions of inclusiveness are not highly politicized and regularized within the organization. In contrast to this, advocacy groups emerging out of progressive social movements have tended in recent years to focus considerable attention on questions of inclusiveness and, in some cases, they have changed their organizational structures to institutionalize these representational concerns. To understand better the ways in which such groups struggle with issues of inclusiveness, we examine in particular detail the experiences of EGALE and the National Action Committee on the Status of Women.

CASE STUDY: EGALE

EGALE, which stands for Equality for Gays and Lesbians Everywhere, is the most prominent national organization within the Canadian gay and lesbian movement. Miriam Smith (1999) describes this movement as a fractured pan-Canadian network of activists and organizations strategically allied around issues of sexuality. While the movement began to mobilize in the early 1960s, EGALE first emerged as an ad hoc committee out of parliamentary hearings held in 1985 on the inclusion of equality rights in section 15 of the Canadian Charter of Rights and Freedoms. The government's positive response to these lobbying efforts led activists to transform the group into a permanent organization. From the beginning, EGALE saw itself as an Ottawa-based group with a national mandate. Its efforts were focused on lobbying the federal government, and it employed its contacts within the bureaucracy and political parties to promote a rights-based agenda. It also engaged in Charter litigation on issues of sexual orientation.

In its first four years of operation, EGALE remained relatively small, with about one hundred supporters and a dozen active volunteers in Ottawa. This created an image of the group as a closed club, a perception strengthened by the composition of the membership: most members were white male professionals located in the Ottawa-Hull region. The group operated without a formal structure and had limited success in its efforts to broaden its membership base. But because EGALE was located in Ottawa, focused on rights issues, and had ties to the media and the federal government, the organization was frequently called on to represent the diverse interests and views of lesbian, gay, bisexual, and transgendered Canadians. As it gained prominence, issues of representation and inclusiveness became a source of tension within the group, and within the broader gay and lesbian rights movement.

These pressures led the group to develop a mission statement that acknowledged the diversity of the lesbian, gay, bisexual, and transgendered communities in Canada, and a set of formal rules governing the conduct of the organization. Combined with efforts to expand the membership, this resulted in an increase in members from 80 in April of 1994 to 565 in 1995 (Smith 2000, 7). In the face of criticisms that the group was unrepresentative of regional diversity and the lesbian community, EGALE revised its internal structure significantly in 1997. The new regional structure required that one man and one woman be elected from each of six regions. In the same reorganization, a francophone caucus was formed for the purpose of lobbying francophone MPs. The 1992 and 1997 reorganizations made EGALE a more representative organization than it had been in its early days. Despite these attempts to become more inclusive, as of 1999, women still constituted a minority (30 percent) of the organization's membership, there were few members from either Alberta or Quebec, and francophones were still underrepresented (Smith 2000, 8). The experience of EGALE demonstrates the added pressures to be internally inclusive faced by organizations with agendas that promote inclusion.

CASE STUDY: NAC

The National Action Committee on the Status of Women (NAC) has an organizational structure very different from EGALE's. Individuals do not participate directly; rather, NAC is an umbrella organization of over 600 women's groups. This umbrella structure, the group's stature as the leading organization representing Canadian women, and the feminist movement's emphasis on inclusion of the most disadvantaged women have combined to make questions of representation and inclusion tremendously important and contentious for NAC.

NAC was originally formed in 1972 to lobby for implementation of the recommendations of the Royal Commission on the Status of Women. Initially it had about forty member groups representing both traditional and feminist organizations. At NAC's founding conference in 1972, organizers "acknowledge[d], and expressed regret at the under-representation of some groups of women. Few women with disabilities participated. While individual women of colour and immigrant women attended, there is no evidence that they did so representing groups from their own communities. The presence of open lesbians was muted. Though delegates attended from every province and territory, there was a preponderance of women from Ontario" (Molgat and Cummings 2003).

Over its thirty years of operation, NAC has tried to address these various issues of inclusion. Linguistic and regional representation were the first contentious lines of cleavage to emerge. NAC's origins were largely in the English Canadian women's movement centred in Toronto, and since its inception the organization has struggled to expand beyond this basis. Linguistic accommodation was addressed four years after NAC was founded, when it began to offer simultaneous interpretation at its meetings; three years later it began to translate its documents into French as well (Molgat and Cummings 2003). In the early 1980s, NAC adopted a new constitution that recognized French and English as "official" languages of the organization, thereby mandating simultaneous interpretation at annual general meetings and translation of all official documents (Vickers, Rankin, and Appelle 1993, 286). These measures, which are the bare minimum for an organization to be functionally bilingual, required considerable funding. However, NAC's relationship to francophone women's organizations has been troubled. The most prominent Quebec feminist organization – la Fédération des femmes de Québec – withdrew from NAC twice in the 1980s in part over disputes regarding NAC's stance on the Meech Lake Accord. As Vickers, Rankin, and Appelle (1993, 286) conclude, "Efforts to make the participation of francophones in NAC meaningful and not just symbolic had limited success." In recent years, these efforts have become less evident as the organization lacks the federal government funding that once subsidized the costs of translation.

NAC has also struggled to achieve meaningful representation for women living outside central Canada. In the first years after it was formed, NAC tried to achieve representation from outside Ontario on its executive, but had trouble recruiting women to hold the positions and for some time could not reimburse regional representatives for the costs of attending meetings. In the 1980s NAC added regional representatives to its executive, and was able to pay their travel costs. Despite these measures, the organization has had difficulty filling these positions for a variety of reasons. Vickers, Rankin, and Appelle (1993, 286) note that feminist organizations in different parts of the country operate in very different contexts, mobilize at different rates, and in some cases are not focused on the federal state. As a result of these factors, as well as the organization's other problems in the late 1990s and early 2000s, almost all the regional representative positions on the NAC executive were vacant as of 2003 and had been for several years.

NAC has been more successful in its efforts to be inclusive of visible minority women. When NAC was first founded, the composition of its executive and active membership was almost exclusively white. It was not until 1979 that a visible minority woman was elected to the national executive. A significant milestone for ethnic inclusivity in the organization came in 1985 when the Visible Minority and Immigrant Women's Committee was formed within NAC. This remains an active committee, reflecting the significant role visible minority women now play within the organization, including holding the presidency of the organization for most of the past decade. NAC has employed affirmative action techniques internally to ensure that visible minority and First Nations women are represented on the group's executive. First Nations women, lesbians, and young women all form caucuses within the organization, and are active on issues specific to their interests. As the organization has become more inclusive for visible minority women, however, some white women have become alienated from the group. As Molgat and Cummings (2003) note, "The failure of some feminists to understand the interconnectedness of dealing with racism as part of feminism led them to withhold financial and other support from NAC."

This brief summary shows that questions of inclusiveness have been a source of considerable difficulty for NAC. This is not surprising, given the broad-based nature of NAC's membership. NAC's problems illustrate two of the reasons questions of inclusion are so difficult for large organizations. First, it is extremely costly to maintain a bilingual, regionally representative organization in a country with the small population and large geography of Canada. These two aspects of inclusiveness alone are virtually insurmountable for a group without an extensive base of funding. Second, the complexity and diversity of Canadian society create profound challenges for groups that seek to be internally inclusive. Much of NAC's history has centred on disputes over questions of inclusiveness. This reflects both the complexity of the task NAC set out for itself as an organization representing Canadian women, and the organization's ideological commitment to achieving inclusiveness. NAC's difficulties in this regard illustrate the enormity of this challenge.

BARRIERS TO ACHIEVING INCLUSIVENESS

The experiences of EGALE and NAC demonstrate that internal structures guaranteeing inclusiveness in the composition of executive bodies are a necessary, but insufficient, condition for achieving inclusive organizations. Even when organizations are genuinely committed to becoming inclusive, significant obstacles can stand in the way of achieving this goal. When it comes to regional inclusiveness, lack of money is a significant barrier: substantial costs are entailed when representatives of far-flung regions have to attend executive meetings. Even conference calls are expensive and are often an inadequate substitute for face-to-face meetings. Linguistic inclusiveness is also expensive, particularly when it comes to providing simultaneous interpretation of meetings. In the absence of government funding, most national organizations cannot afford these expenditures.

Achieving inclusiveness along lines of gender, ethnicity, sexual orientation, and ability is even more challenging. These aspects of identity, like language and to a lesser degree region, are sources of profound social and political difference. Accommodating diversity within an organization requires more than guaranteeing seats on an executive body. It demands a rethinking of an organization's ways of approaching issues and making decisions. It forces dedicated, long-time activists to create space in an organization for people with whom they may not be comfortable and who may bring new concerns to the table that crowd out traditional issues. As NAC's experience in recent years illustrates vividly, organizations can have trouble maintaining their "mainstream" core of activists when the organization becomes more inclusive of societal diversity. This entails significant costs for the organization in terms of its basis of support and ability to intervene effectively in public forums. Attention to issues of inclusiveness clearly presents significant challenges to a group's ability to adopt unified positions in its negotiations with government. The costs may in fact be so great that they entirely incapacitate the group. Nonetheless, from an Audit perspective, it is a positive development that groups in the progressive social movement sector perceive social inclusiveness as a desirable objective.

The most negative development in terms of groups' capacity to be inclusive lies in the sharp decline in government funding facilitating the operation of bilingual, pan-Canadian organizations. The bilingual and federal character of Canada, combined with its vast geography, poses special problems for Canadian groups. Government has a role to play in facilitating inclusive national organizations under such conditions. This is a theme we return to in Chapter 5.

Participation

In Chapter 3, we demonstrated that citizens who belong to groups are generally more satisfied with Canadian democracy and more inclined toward active citizenship in other respects. These findings highlight how important it is that groups structure themselves to allow extensive and meaningful individual participation by members. Applying the Audit value of participation to the internal life of groups, two dimensions of participation come into play. The first relates to the openness of group membership, and the second to what kinds of participatory opportunities are offered to group members.

When we think about the democratic ideal with respect to group participation, the first impulse is to argue that more is better. Groups with more members engage a larger number of Canadians in a participatory experience than groups with fewer members, and have a better chance of accurately representing the views of their constituencies. Similarly, groups that offer their members many opportunities to participate in decision making more closely approximate the democratic ideal and are more likely to be responsive to their constituencies. However, trade-offs are inherent in the relationship between size of membership and the extent to which individual group members can participate in group decision making. Groups struggle to find a balance between these two competing values. To better understand these trade-offs, we examine the spectrum of models of both openness and extent of participation for a number of Canadian groups.

Openness

As groups constitute themselves, one of the first decisions they have to make relates to who is eligible to join their group. Is membership to be limited, or can anyone join? Many groups have little reason to consider limiting membership, because they gain legitimacy and revenues from a large membership. Examples of broad membership organizations that operate on this logic include the Council of Canadians, the Canadian Automobile Association, and numerous university student unions or associations. The Council of Canadians claims to be Canada's pre-eminent citizens' watchdog organization, with over 100,000 members across the country. The cost of membership is a donation of at least $35 (or $6 for individuals on fixed incomes), which entitles a member to vote at the organization's annual general meeting. The Canadian Automobile Association is a rather different case, as members usually join it to benefit from the services it provides, not to endorse the organization as a lobby group. The CAA boasts over four million members nationwide, making it one of the country's largest interest groups in terms of membership. A third model is that of university student associations, in which membership is usually compulsory for all undergraduate students. Once student associations have been voted into existence by a majority of students, they can require all students to pay membership fees in return for which they get a range of services, including having the association lobby governments on their behalf.

Large membership-based advocacy organizations are fairly rare in Canada, at least at the national level. When we look at the range of groups active in lobbying the federal government, membership-based organizations appear to be the exception rather than the rule. Many of the organizations active at the national level are coalitions of other groups, some of which have individual members. To the extent that these coalitions are made up of membership groups, they still create participatory opportunities.

The question of openness of membership can be particularly thorny for groups representing a constituency with a shared ascriptive characteristic. Should sympathetic men be welcomed as members of a women's lobby group? Should parents of people with mental illness be permitted to join a group representing people with mental illness? Should middle-class professional social workers be allowed to join antipoverty organizations speaking for poor people? Groups deal with these issues in a variety of ways, often on an ad hoc basis. One resolution of this issue that maximizes participation while recognizing the need for self-determination is the rule adopted by the Coalition of Provincial Organizations of the Handicapped that any group joining its coalition be at least 51 percent controlled by people with disabilities.

At the other end of the spectrum are organizations that choose to keep their memberships limited. Reasons for this vary: some may wish to make the group exclusive and therefore desirable. For example, membership in the Council of Canadian Chief Executives is limited to the chief executive officers of major Canadian corporations. The group's claim to represent the very upper echelons of Canadian business would clearly be weakened if its membership were open to executives of lesser enterprises. Other groups choose to remain small so that they can pursue their policy activities with maximum flexibility. An example of this would be the Toronto group People for Education, which began as a group of twelve women who deliberately kept their group small because growth would require adopting structure which, in turn, would reduce the group's flexibility (Falconer 2001, 87).

A growing number of Canadian advocacy groups have opted not to have members at all. Organizations like Greenpeace Canada, the Canadian Taxpayers Federation, and Environment Voters welcome "supporters," who give the organization money, but do not have members. The distinction between supporters and members is crucial: supporters have no direct input into the group's direction, while members are entitled, at a minimum, to vote in elections for an organization's board of directors. We refer to groups that have only supporters, but not members, as staff-led organizations. This term reflects the professionalization of these groups, which rely on paid staff both to undertake advocacy work and to maintain the ongoing fundraising initiatives that keep them in operation.

Why would the founders or leaders of groups choose to construct a staff-led organization? The first, and most significant, reason has to do with control. A membership organization is vulnerable to takeover by its opponents. For instance, forestry workers' unions have tried to stage takeovers of membership-based environmental groups that opposed logging. Even like-minded, well-intentioned members can decide to push an organization in a direction its leaders or staff see as strategically inappropriate or peripheral to the group's mandate. Doing away with membership eliminates these kinds of threats. The second reason group founders and leaders opt not to form membership organizations reflects a calculation that members are simply more trouble than they are worth. Maintaining an active membership organization is costly and time-consuming. If group leaders and staff are able to obtain money from supporters without incurring the costs of maintaining a membership organization, it is rational for them to do so.

From an Audit perspective, the trend toward memberless organizations is troubling. As we discuss below, this trend significantly limits the potential for citizens to engage in meaningful political participation through advocacy group membership.

EXTENT OF PARTICIPATION

The second aspect of participation involves the opportunities offered to group members. Once again, Canadian groups differ vastly in this regard. The two basic models are the participatory membership organization, at one end of the spectrum, and the staff- or executive-led organization, at the nonparticipatory end of the continuum. The former has members, while the latter has financial supporters. Although there are no comprehensive studies of group organization, our cursory examination suggests that in Canada, as elsewhere, staff-led organizations are becoming the predominant model, at least at the national level.

Participatory organizations create opportunities for their members to engage in the group's governance and decision making. At a minimum, they are governed by an executive elected by the membership. Closer to the democratic ideal, however, are those organizations that offer their members extensive opportunities for involvement in charting the group's course. While it is feasible for a community-based organization with a relatively small membership to involve its members in decision making, few large national organizations do so because of the practical barriers of cost and complexity, particularly when their membership is spread across the country. One group leader we spoke to suggested that a group must have at least 100,000 members before direct member involvement in the form of voting on resolutions or other issues is financially viable. Many groups may simply lack the capacity to consult regularly with their members: in a survey of leaders of civil society organizations, Embuldeniya (2001, vi) found that 57 percent of respondents believed that large umbrella organizations representing coalitions of smaller, local groups, or even national organizations sharing an interest on an issue, are unable to represent the interests of their members. They were, however, more optimistic about the ability of smaller local organizations to build strong relationships with their stakeholders: 68 percent believed that civil society organizations involve constituents, stakeholders, and volunteers in planning, designing, and implementing processes.

Changes in communication technologies have the potential to lower the costs for groups to consult with their members. The Internet and e-mail allow groups to communicate with their members quickly and relatively easily. Craig Jones of the BC Civil Liberties Association notes that the Internet enabled his group to "communicate very effectively amongst ourselves and with the media. We could let a select two hundred people know of a piece of news or ask them a question, and within minutes or hours at the most, get an answer back" (in Falconer 2001, 39). Several cross-national lobbying campaigns, including the notable mobilization to defeat the Multilateral Agreement on Investment (MAI), have been coordinated over the Internet.

Even more significant than the costs entailed by involving members directly in decision making are the constraints this places on group leaders. With no members, organizations have considerable strategic room for manoeuvre. As Annie Kidder says of People for Education, "We aren't democratic, we're not representative, we're not elected. It leaves us completely free" (in Falconer 2001, 87). Without the consideration of consulting members, group leaders are able to respond quickly to government requests for consultations, or to government announcements of policy. They are also free to direct the group's strategic plan according to the political opportunities and barriers they perceive. In short, strategic flexibility is maximized in such arrangements.

One organization that has achieved an admirable balance between group leaders' imperative for autonomy and the desire to allow members to participate actively and direct the group's policy interventions is the Council of Canadians. Members have the right to vote for an executive and on policy-related resolutions at an annual general meeting. In reality, however, since the membership is spread across the country and the annual meeting is held in one location (which rotates around the country), individual members have a limited opportunity to direct the national organization's policy. The Council's structure nonetheless provides local chapters with considerable autonomy to pursue the issues they think are important as long as they fall within the national group's general mandate. Following essentially a franchise model, the national organization distributes materials to help chapters form, operate, and engage in effective advocacy activities. It also provides occasional funding for chapters' advocacy activities. In this way, members are actively engaged but the national organization maintains strategic autonomy.

Groups that have emerged from progressive social movements face a particular pressure to be participatory in their internal structures and practices. Embedded in the ideological content of social movements like the women's movement, the peace movement, and the environmental movement is a critique of hierarchical structures (which would include those of staff-led organizations) and a clear preference for egalitarian, participatory democracy.

In staff or executive-led organizations, decisions regarding the group's policy stances, strategies, and tactics are made by professional staff members or the group's executive. Supporters have little or no influence over the group's direction. Not surprisingly, most business and industry associations fit into this category, since they exist not as participatory organizations but rather to pursue their constituents' economic interests in the most efficient manner possible. Following this model, the Canadian Council of Chief Executives has a permanent chief executive officer who is the public face of the organization. The high-flying CEOs who constitute the organization's membership meet only once or twice a year to give policy guidance. Similarly, industry associations tend to have professionalized staff who take direction from an elected board of directors. In his 1988 study of business organizations, Coleman found that most of these boards were selected informally. Board members were usually elected at the association's annual general meeting, but "the elections are often ratifications of an executive already formed behind the scenes," ensuring representation from the largest firms in the association's domain (Coleman 1988, 33).

Staff-led organizations that have only supporters, not members, offer very limited opportunities for citizen involvement. From an Audit perspective, the rise of memberless, staff-led organizations is a source of considerable concern. These national-level groups are apparently flourishing to the detriment of smaller and more local groups. They are run out of central locations by paid staff who often have marketing or business backgrounds. They are more concerned with "branding" their organizations than with engaging citizens in participatory processes. In most cases the relationship between members and the group is purely financial (Maloney and Jordan 1997; Putnam 2000; Stanbury 2000). Writing about this phenomenon in the United States, Robert Putnam (1995, 71) has argued that "for the vast majority of their members, the only act of membership consists in writing a cheque for dues or perhaps occasionally reading a newsletter. Few ever attend any meetings of such organizations, and most are unlikely ever (knowingly) to encounter any other member."

Because supporters are typically drawn into the group through direct mail campaigns and usually remain connected to the organization only through its requests for financial donations or membership renewals, these groups often have a high turnover in "membership." These groups tend to be hierarchal in nature, creating vertical links between members and the national organization, and connecting members to "common symbols, common leaders, and perhaps common ideals, but not to one another" (Putnam 1995, 71). As a consequence, democratic participation in which citizens interact and debate with one another is abandoned in favour of a form of participation by proxy in which citizens delegate their responsibilities to professional negotiating institutions (Maloney 1999, 111). This minimal relationship with members also has serious implications for the accountability of these groups, as will be discussed below under the heading "Responsiveness."

Staff-led groups clearly provide few opportunities for members to be actively involved in the organization's policy development. Either supporters cannot vote at annual general meetings, or it is difficult for members to exercise any such entitlement. That said, not all authors are as critical of chequebook participation as a mode of citizen activity. In one view, it encourages citizens to take an interest in politics, which is important in a democratic society (Maloney 1999). It also reduces many of the entrance barriers to group participation by reducing the effort needed by citizens to identify groups that may represent their issues and concerns and to determine how to join (Goodwin 1988). Once individuals have become members they may then be asked to participate in more demanding activities such as attending rallies, writing letters, or even showing up to meetings on behalf of the organization. As Maloney (1999, 117) has concluded, "While cheque-writers' contribution may in fact be small, it is certainly better than not participating at all ... It may be a supplementary/complementary participatory activity to more active political involvement, or at least of a similar level of commitment as voting in liberal democracies."

The simple act of writing a cheque is certainly preferable to disengaging entirely from political life. In our ideal democracy, advocacy groups would be organized so as to engage citizens in a participatory form of democratic activity. In the real world of Canadian society, however, many citizens feel they do not have enough time to participate extensively in such organizations. The general trend in advanced industrialized societies is toward specialization and professionalization. Rather than volunteering their time in support of a political campaign or cause, citizens in these societies increasingly vote with their wallets, paying professionals in staff-led organizations to advocate on their behalf. This has led to the professionalization not only of advocacy groups but also of political parties (see Cross 2004). As we discuss in Chapters 5 through 8, advocacy groups have an important role to play in the development of public policy in Canada. Without money, they cannot fulfill this role. In this respect, staff-led organizations are preferable to an absence of voices in policy debates. While we accept staff-led organizations as a necessary adaptation to changing circumstances, we nonetheless maintain that the model of local activism and autonomy adopted by the Council of Canadians could serve as a model for staff-led organizations that want to develop an activist base and thereby strengthen democratic citizenship in Canada.

Responsiveness

In the context of groups' internal affairs, the Audit value of responsiveness refers to how accountable the leaders and staff of groups are to their members, supporters, and constituency. Each of these three components require distinct relationships of accountability, and must be discussed separately. Our primary focus will be on the ways in which groups try to respond to the policy preferences of their grassroots, with a secondary focus on the mechanisms through which group leaders and staffs can be held accountable.

The issue of group leaders' responsiveness is centrally important for an audit of groups' relationship to democracy. As we noted in Chapter 2, one of the core critiques levelled at groups is that they are unaccountable bodies representing "special interests." As Susan Phillips (1995, 4-5) notes, "Representation by groups of citizens is under attack in Canada. Citizen groups engaged in any form of advocacy have been dismissed in recent years as 'special interest groups,' implying that they are narrow-minded and wholly self-interested. It has become common for politicians and the media to question whether the leadership of voluntary organizations truly represents the memberships and the constituencies on whose behalf they purport to speak." This critique strikes at the very legitimacy of groups' participation in the democratic process, and as such requires careful consideration.

Responsiveness to Members

The least demanding dimension of responsiveness involves accountability of group leaders to group members. This kind of accountability presupposes that just as citizenship entitles individuals to exercise control over elected officials in the broader democratic system, membership in an organization entitles members to participate in group decision making. Mechanisms for exerting this control include participating in setting policy, having opportunities to ask group leaders about the group's policies, strategies, and tactics, and ultimately being able to call leaders to account through regular elections to the group's executive. We suspect that such relationships of accountability are the exception rather than the rule among Canadian advocacy groups.

The category "responsiveness to members" presupposes that a group does in fact have members. As we have seen in this chapter, this assumption frequently does not hold true. At the national, and even provincial, levels, many advocacy groups are umbrella-type structures. While these are effective modes of organization for pursuing policy objectives, they pose difficulties for achieving relationships of accountability. An illustration of this is the Canadian Federation of Students (CFS), an umbrella organization encompassing over sixty university and college students' associations. While the group claims to represent over 400,000 postsecondary students, its relationship with them is only indirect: students elect the leadership of their institution's student union, and these leaders participate in selecting the leadership and directing the affairs of the CFS. Students who disagree with the direction of the CFS have no recourse but either to run for student government or to lobby to pull out of the national coalition. Thus, the relationship of accountability is indirect. This situation is not unique to the CFS: other major national organizations such as the Assembly of First Nations and NAC share the same basic organizational form.

Staff-led groups also offer few participatory opportunities to their members and hence have little chance to respond to them. In large organizations that afford members few formal entitlements to shape the groups' direction, group leaders often use surveys of all or part of the membership (or donor base) as a basis for determining policy stands. For instance, the Canadian Automobile Association surveys a random sample of its over four million members, seeking their opinions on issues of interest to the car-driving public. The group then uses this survey as a basis for its core policy document, which is distributed to provincial and federal politicians as well as public servants (CAA

2003). Such a survey provides at least some legitimacy for the organization's claims to represent the auto-driving public. However, surveys can only solicit members' opinions on the issues that the group's leadership has decided are important. They offer little or no opportunity for group members to raise other issues or suggest a shift in focus or tactics for the group. If members do not like the positions that the group is advocating they have little option but to stop contributing money to the group (Stanbury 2000). Yet as Maloney and Jordan (1997, 117) point out, "These (successful) protest businesses do not *naïvely* lead and *hope* that members will follow. As sensible businesses they have done their market research (e.g., via membership surveys) and know what members can 'live with.'" In the absence of members, the only relationships of accountability relevant to these organizations are accountability to supporters and to constituency.

RESPONSIVENESS TO SUPPORTERS

For groups without a formal membership, responsiveness involves finding ways for group leaders to consult with Canadians who are supportive of their cause. In the absence of explicit relationships of accountability, the only mechanism making group leaders responsive to supporters is money. If a group relies on supporters for a significant portion of its funds, its financial survival depends upon maintaining the support of donors. Money is not a trivial mechanism of accountability: if an organization strays too far from the issues its supporters care about, or if it adopts tactics its supporters disapprove of, the group stands to lose its livelihood.

That said, the scrutiny of group supporters should not be overemphasized. Many, if not most, of these supporters are responding to direct mail appeals from the organization, and may well be swayed by the content of the appeal. Direct-mail fundraisers emphasize clear, simple messages in their appeals, and craft letters to evoke emotional responses of fear, anger, or sympathy. For instance, in the course of writing this book, one of the authors received a direct mail solicitation from the Canadian Taxpayers Federation. The heading of the letter was "Taxation According to Race?" and the gist of the appeal for funds was that a court decision exempting First Nations covered by Treaty 8 from paying taxes could yield a precedent resulting in "taxes being applied in Canada on the basis of racial ancestry." The letter oversimplified the issue and tried to invoke racial tension. Such appeals allow organizations to raise the funds they need to operate. But to the extent that supporters are responding to these simple, emotive appeals, they are doing little to hold group leaders accountable. In essence, the direct mail game does not reward groups for moderation, even-handedness, or thorough presentation of relevant information.

Moreover, as Stanbury (2000) points out, the relationship of financial accountability to supporters breaks down when groups are able to obtain funds from other sources. Government funding, grants from foundations, transfers from international branches of their organization, or support from other institutions like churches, unions, or corporations can allow groups to remain in operation even when their other supporters abandon them. Under these circumstances, accountability to supporters becomes a problematic concept.

Does this mean that staff-led groups, particularly those that receive funding from sources other than their supporters, do not have a legitimate role to play in discussions of public policy? Any citizen is entitled to make a case to government, and unrepresentative groups should be no different. Groups that lack mechanisms of accountability can contribute to the public debate by providing information and articulating a coherent point of view. What they cannot do is claim to represent a significant segment of the population. As long as groups are transparent about their lack of representative capacity, their participation in the public debate is legitimate. That said, decision makers must be careful to distinguish between groups that have genuine representative capacity and those that do not. This is an issue that we return to in the concluding chapter.

Responsiveness to Constituency

The third, and most difficult, level of responsiveness involves accountability to the constituency a group purports to represent. If advocacy groups claim to represent collectivities like "drivers," "women," "nonsmokers," or "the disabled," questions are raised regarding the veracity of these claims. The larger and the more diverse the collectivity the group purports to represent, the more problematic the claim becomes.

From our review of case studies of interest-group decision-making practices, it appears that group leaders and staffs often enjoy considerable autonomy in setting their organization's priorities and policy stances. In many cases, group leaders use their judgment and knowledge of their constituency to determine the group's actions. For instance, Boyce et al. (2001, 150-1) find that among the groups included in their study of advocacy in the disability field, "consumer groups attempt to achieve the democratic principles of representativeness by focusing on a broad range of activities that are important to all or most persons with disabilities, rather than by formally recruiting a broad range of people to participate. This strategy ... assumes that differences among people with disabilities are not as great as differences between access to activities by persons with disabilities and by able-bodied persons."

Such approaches are fraught with potential difficulties. A vivid illustration of this is offered by NAC's interventions into policy consultations over assisted reproductive technologies (ARTs; Fortier, Montpetit, and Scala 2003). NAC first intervened in the public debate over ARTs in 1990 with a presentation to a royal commission studying the issue. In preparing this presentation, NAC followed what Fortier, Montpetit, and Scala call "the logic of delegation based on identity" (8). NAC did not consult with its member groups in formulating its stance; rather, "it was a product of several other factors, including its practice of delegating research work to committees made up of experts or activists in a particular policy area" (9). NAC's submission to the royal commission also "reflected the NAC's decision to evaluate policy issues in terms of their impact on the most disadvantaged women" (ibid.). The resulting report was highly critical of all ARTs, largely on the grounds that these technologies "could only serve to maintain women's subordinate position in society by expanding opportunities for women's exploitation and oppression" (8). NAC's unflinchingly oppositional stance toward ARTs drew a great deal of criticism from individuals and women's groups that rejected NAC's efforts to "advance a universal feminist perspective on the issue of ARTs" (9). In particular, lesbians and infertile women who stood to benefit from these technologies in their quest to have biological children rejected NAC's stance and threw into question NAC's legitimacy as a representative organization of Canadian women. Thus groups that purport to speak for a collectivity may encounter trouble if they do so based on research and analysis rather than extensive consultations with their members and constituents.

The second part of the story of NAC's involvement in the ART policy arena illustrates another difficulty facing advocacy groups: extensive consultations with a diverse constituency can make it impossible for a group to intervene effectively in the policy process. In the aftermath of the royal commission, NAC's representatives decided that they could not speak on behalf of women without consultation. But these consultations left NAC unable to develop a consensus position. Its brief on legislation intended to regulate ARTs stated, "As an organization we do not have consensus about the best models for ensuring equality of result," and did not clearly state whether the organization believed the legislation should be enacted as law (Fortier, Montpetit, and Scala 2003, 12). Consequently, NAC could not exert any influence over the outcome of the legislative process. This example illustrates the tension between effective advocacy, on the one hand, and responsiveness to a group's constituency, on the other.

Although generalizations about the extent to which organizations are representative of their constituencies are impossible, organizations with substantial membership bases and methods for consulting those members are better positioned to make claims that they are representative of their constituencies. Efforts to consult widely within constituencies can certainly produce more representative policy stances. Once again, we believe the onus is on government decision makers to weigh the claims of advocacy groups based in part on their capacity to represent their constituency. This would create an incentive for group leaders to remain responsive both to members and broader constituencies.

Evaluating the Internal Life of Groups

Canadian groups vary widely in their efforts to be inclusive, provide participatory opportunities for their members, and be responsive to their members, supporters, and constituencies. Some organizations approach the democratic ideal in these respects, while others fall far short. A number of barriers stand in the way of groups constituting themselves as inclusive, participatory organizations. Money is a significant factor for many groups: building inclusive, participatory organizations, particularly at the national level, is an expensive undertaking that some organizations lack the financial capacity to achieve. Extensive membership involvement can also have the paradoxical effect of decreasing a group's capacity to respond quickly as opportunities open up in the policy cycle.

As we saw in Chapter 3, active membership in advocacy groups is correlated with other desirable aspects of citizenship, including propensity to vote, to trust other citizens, and to engage with government. Therefore Canadian governments have an interest in helping groups develop the capacity to organize themselves as participatory democratic organizations. They can do this by providing resources directed toward capacity building (an issue discussed in the next chapter) and by demonstrating in the course of public consultations that groups that engage their members in a meaningful way are particularly valued in the policy process, an issue which we return to in Chapter 9.

Chapter 4

Strengths

- Many groups, particularly those linked to equality-seeking movements, try to be inclusive along linguistic, regional, and to a lesser extent gender and ethnic lines.
- Some groups find ways to involve members in decision making and maintain relationships of accountability with members.

Weaknesses

- Groups that are struggling to maintain their organizational effectiveness because of limited funds find It particularly difficult to be either inclusive or participatory in their membership practices.
- The trend toward staff-led organizations that eschew members in favour of supporters limits the potential beneficial impact of group membership for Canadians, and reduces the accountability of organizations to their supporters and constituencies.
- Groups that place greater emphasis on consulting members often face greater challenges in determining cohesive policy goals.

WHICH INTERESTS AND IDENTITIES ARE MOBILIZED?

5

The previous two chapters examined the internal dynamics of advocacy groups from the perspective of democracy. In this chapter, we turn our attention toward the advocacy group system as a whole to determine which interests and identities find representation within the system, and which tend to be left without a voice.

In making this determination, we are focusing on the Audit criterion of inclusiveness. Inclusiveness requires that all relevant interests or identities be mobilized and given voice in the public sphere. Democracy is not well served if only the affluent, well-educated, able-bodied segments of society have a voice within the group system; an equitable and inclusive conception of democracy requires that marginalized groups also be included in the voices heard in the public arena. In fact, it may be all the more important that marginalized groups be given a voice through the group system, as they tend to be significantly underrepresented in formal legislative and executive bodies (see Docherty 2004 and White 2005).

The question of which interests or identities are politically relevant, or salient, is a thorny one. We all have a myriad of interests based on anything from where we live, whom we live with, how we are employed, the status of our health, to something as simple as the hobbies we pursue. Some of these interests are politically relevant much of the time: for instance, many Canadians perceive their interests as Quebeckers or Westerners as highly relevant, and these regional interests consistently shape their political attitudes and behaviour. Other interests remain latent for years, becoming politicized only as a result of a public policy initiative or other circumstance. For example, people who hunt for sport would not have thought of their hobby as a politically relevant interest until the federal government introduced legislation requiring them to register their firearms, at which time many gun owners mobilized into advocacy groups to try to reverse the government's decision.

The mobilization of identities is even more complex: all of us have many potential identities based in our ascriptive characteristics: we are working class or middle class, men or women, gay or straight, Eastern or Western, right-handed or left-handed. For these identities to become politically salient, what is usually required is the emergence of a social movement to make the claim that this identity matters. If it were not for the activities of the labour movement, the women's movement, the gay rights movement, and Western populist movements in the past, the distinctions between different classes, genders and the like would seem as politically meaningless as the distinction between left- and right-handed people.

What factors determine whether a group is mobilized? The most influential theoretical perspective on this question is offered by Mancur Olson (1965), who first articulated the "free rider problem." Olson argues that people have no incentive to participate in political action if they can be "free riders" and benefit from the outcome without joining in the mobilization. For example, imagine that a university student association is holding a rally to try to convince the government to increase funding for universities in order to make tuition fees lower. A "rational" student might calculate that the cost of attending the rally (such as hours of study lost) is greater than the marginal difference that her participation in the rally would make. Any benefits that accrue from the rally in the form of lower tuition would not be limited to those who attended the rally, so her best interest would lie in being a free rider on the efforts of the other, less calculating, students.

Two propositions follow from Olson's rational choice analysis of group mobilization. First, we are more likely to see groups mobilize in pursuit of selective benefits that accrue only to their members, such as profits for business or monetary rewards for members of the group. Groups are less likely to mobilize in pursuit of collective benefits that accrue to everyone, such as clean air or justice. Second, people have greater incentive to mobilize around narrower interests, like a tax break for a certain group, than diffuse interests, such as lower costs for a relatively minor consumer good.

A second theoretical perspective suggests that resources are the greatest constraint on the mobilization of groups. Resources – which include time, money, status, skills, and confidence – are required in order to form groups and take public stands. Segments of society that lack several of these resources are less likely to mobilize than those that have access to them. Compounding this, many of these sets of resources tend to correlate with one another: affluent people are more likely to have the formal education that hones their skills in presenting their case in public, which in turn gives them both the social status and the confidence to pursue their interests in the public arena. We have already seen some evidence of this tendency in our audit. In Chapter 3, we reported that members of advocacy groups tended to be older, middle class, and from majority ethnic groups.

Even in social movements, which are often portrayed as emerging to better the situation of marginalized groups, studies find that access to resources is a key predictor of movement mobilization. The most downtrodden groups seldom mobilize: it is not until members of the group start to accrue some resources, whether in the form of money, education, or self-confidence, that mobilization occurs. For instance, African Americans did not organize to combat segregation until an educated African American middle class emerged and provided leaders to the movement. Women did not start questioning their second-class place in Canadian society until many of them had pursued university education and professional careers in the 1960s. It follows from this that groups representing relatively well-off citizens are more likely to emerge than are groups representing the marginalized citizens most in need of a voice in the political arena.

Clearly, these theoretical perspectives offer pessimistic predictions about the capacity of the advocacy group/social movement system to meet the democratic criterion of inclusiveness. However, other factors can interfere with the behaviours predicted by theoretical models of human behaviour. Some Canadians may not base their political activities on a strict rational calculus, choosing instead to pursue their vision of the common good. Marginalized segments of society may find ways to overcome their lack of resources and mobilize despite their disadvantages. In addition, as we will see, these theoretical perspectives do not take the state into account. In Canada, the federal government has historically played a significant and conscious role in trying to remedy some of the inequities that follow from the behaviours predicted by these theories.

Free Riders and Diffuse Interests

We start our audit of the inclusiveness of the advocacy group system in Canada by considering whether the expectations of rational choice theory are borne out in the Canadian experience. First, do most groups active in the Canadian advocacy group system pursue selective benefits (i.e., benefits that accrue only to group members)? Certainly many of the active groups fall into this category. A 1995 survey of associations in Canada found that, excluding leisure groups like sports clubs, only 16 percent of associations could be classified as "public interest" groups. More common were industry and trade associations (32 percent), groups focused on the welfare and protection of individuals (28 percent), and unions (24 percent) (Amara, Landry, and Lamari 1999, 483). These findings lend weight to the assertion that groups pursuing selective benefits mobilize more readily.

The most obvious instances of groups pursuing selective benefits are businesses, which are seeking to maximize their profits. Businesses are well represented within the Canadian advocacy group system. In addition to several major national lobby groups for business such as the Council of Chief Executives, the Canadian Chamber of Commerce, and the Canadian Federation of Independent Business, at least 400 trade associations operate in Canada, each of them representing the interests of either one industry or a subsection of an industry (Brooks and Stritch 1991, 220-1). Pursuing even more selective benefits are the many medium-sized and large corporations that employ government relations specialists to represent their own interests with government. As of July 2002 there were 152 companies with executives or government relations specialists registered as lobbyists at the federal level alone.

There are, however, also many groups pursuing the public interest as they perceive it, in the form of collective goods. For instance, hundreds, if not thousands, of environmental groups seek to improve the quality of the air we all breathe and the water we all drink; their members would not derive any greater benefit from such improvements than would any other member of society, although they might get greater satisfaction from the change. Numerous other groups mobilize to advocate for their vision of the public interest, whether it involves · peace, limiting access to abortion, or ending child poverty. These groups pursuing collective goods are joined by many other groups advocating a version of the public interest that they believe would ameliorate the condition of their segment of society. For example, antipoverty activists advocate changes to public policy that would benefit poorer people at the expense of the wealthy, and taxpayers' groups advocate lower income taxes that would offer the greatest benefits to higher income earners. These groups are not pursuing selective benefits in that the changes they seek would not be limited to group members, but rather would accrue to all low-income or high-income Canadians.

The second prediction of the rational choice theory of advocacy group formation suggests that it is easier to mobilize around narrower interests than diffuse issues (those that affect a large number of people in a relatively minor way). In discussing the mobilization of diffuse interests, a commonly employed example is consumers of a common, but fairly inexpensive, good such as telephone service. Almost every Canadian household has a telephone, so there is a universal interest in relatively low-cost telephone service. Telephone consumers are a diffuse interest not just because the interest is universal, but also because few individuals are concerned enough about the cost of their telephone service to be willing to become active on the issue. Under these circumstances, is it possible for mobilization to occur to represent this interest?

In the Canadian experience, the answer to this is a tentative yes. Until fairly recently, both local and long-distance telephone services in Canada were delivered by companies with provincial monopolies. These companies were regulated by the Canadian Radio-television and Telecommunications Commission (CRTC). Until the 1960s, consumers had virtually no voice within this regulatory process. The advent of consumer representation before the CRTC came not at the instigation of an advocacy group, but on the initiative of the federal Department of Consumer and Corporate Affairs. Government officials encouraged an existing advocacy group, the Consumers' Association of Canada, to become involved in the regulation of telecommunications, and offered the group funding to pursue this role starting in 1973. The CAC remained an active participant in telecommunications regulatory activity until the early 1990s when its federal government funding for such advocacy work was ended. In addition to losing its government funding, deregulation of long-distance service made it more difficult for the CAC to identify a single consumer interest in this field; the interests of more affluent consumers who frequently used long-distance service were pitted against the interests of less wealthy consumers whose greatest interest lay in less expensive local telephone service (see Schultz 2002).

The example of consumer advocacy relating to telecommunications reflects the more general difficulties involved in mobilizing consumers as a group, and the significant role the Canadian government has played in such mobilization. The major voice for Canadian consumers is the Consumers' Association of Canada, which has branches in several provinces as well as its national organization. Formed in 1947 as a volunteer-based nonprofit association, the CAC has in recent decades relied heavily on government funding in order to fulfill its mandate. When governments, particularly the federal government, started to withdraw funding for consumer groups in the early 1990s, the CAC faced financial difficulties. The organization underwent a significant financial crisis in 1993, in part because it had overextended itself trying to offer a consumer magazine to its members (Schultz 2002). The organization received almost $2 million in emergency funding from the federal government at this time, in addition to significant assistance from the Consumers Union of the United States, which forgave outstanding loans to the organization and agreed to include mailings from the CAC to the 200,000 Canadians who subscribed to the Consumers Union magazine, *Consumer Reports* (Schultz 2002, 46; Webb et al. 1996).

In 1998-9 Industry Canada provided only $1 million in total funding for consumer advocacy, distributing this money among nine organizations. The decline in government funding for consumer organizations has prompted a discussion of alternative sources of funding. Ironically, much of this discussion was sponsored by the Office of Consumer Affairs within Industry Canada (see Webb et al. 1996; Webb and Cassells 1995). Among the proposed solutions were a consumers' foundation that could solicit contributions and fund consumer advocacy groups, increased reliance on strategic alliances both among groups and between groups and business, and the development of citizen utility boards. These CUBs are based on an American model in which government requires businesses in certain sectors to include with their monthly billing statements a flyer soliciting membership in a citizens' advocacy group to speak on behalf of consumers in that sector.

Citizen utility boards have been advocated in Canada as a means of overcoming the difficulties involved in developing a self-funding consumers' advocacy group targeting the activities of the banking and financial services sector. The chartered banks enjoy considerable protection from international competition, afforded to them by the federal government. Bank customers constitute a diffuse interest, as most Canadians are customers of a bank, but few voices speak on their behalf when it comes to questions of regulation and bank accountability. On these grounds, a group of advocacy organizations has called for the creation of a citizens' utility board for the financial services industry. The Canadian Community Reinvestment Coalition has advocated that the federal government require banks to include a flyer advertising the formation of such a CUB in their monthly statements to customers. The group estimates that if only 5 percent of bank customers agreed to join at a cost of $20, the CUB would have resources of between $15 and $20 million (CCRC 1997). The federal government has not acted on this issue.

From this brief overview of the organization and activity of consumer groups in Canada over the past three decades, it is clear that mobilization of diffuse interests is in fact very difficult. In the Canadian experience, however, government intervention has been the key to overcoming the inherent difficulties. We will return to the role of the state in overcoming barriers to mobilization later in this chapter.

Limited Resources

The second constraint on mobilization of groups has to do with resources. Are segments of society with limited access to resources – notably money, skills, confidence, and time – less likely than other groups to mobilize to further their political interests? This is an important test, because arguably these marginalized segments of society are most in need of representation in the political sphere. They potentially have the most to gain from positive state action, and they tend not to be well represented within legislatures and other representative bodies (see Docherty 2004; White 2005).

To determine the extent to which lack of resources affects the ability of groups to form, we will examine the mobilization of people living in poverty, who are potentially one of the most difficult groups to organize. People living in poverty by definition lack what many consider to be the most essential element for group mobilization: money. While a group representing middle-class interests could easily expect members to pay a $20 membership fee, or to make larger contributions to sustain the group, such expectations are not realistic for people struggling to meet day-to-day financial needs. In many instances, poverty also correlates with a lack of education, which means that the skills and confidence needed to engage with government may also be less available to these citizens than to others. Moreover, the experience of poverty can erode individuals' sense of self-confidence, with the same result. Given all these factors, people living in poverty are a crucial test case for the proposition that a lack of resources impairs the ability to mobilize. Our analysis in Chapter 3 of who joins groups already showed some evidence of this: only 9 percent of people with household incomes under $60,000 belonged to groups, compared to almost 14 percent with higher household incomes.

A number of antipoverty associations exist in Canada at the local, provincial, and national levels. Some of these organizations are composed of people living in poverty, while others, such as associations of food banks, are organizations that work on their behalf. These organizations range from relatively mainstream lobby-type organizations to radical left-wing groups like the Ontario Coalition Against Poverty, which works on behalf of poor people but also holds demonstrations challenging the capitalist system.

A 1990 study of the antipoverty organizations active at the national level identified six significant groups: the Canadian Council on Social Development (CCSD), the National Council of Welfare Organizations (NCW), the National Anti-Poverty Organization (NAPO), the National Action Committee on the Status of Women (NAC), the National Pensioners and Senior Citizens Federation, and the Canadian Association of Social Workers (Haddow 1990, 227). Of these groups, two represent the interests of segments of society that are more likely to live in poverty – women and seniors – and are not specifically antipoverty organizations. The Canadian Association of Social Workers represents professionals employed in the field, but does not directly represent the interests of poor people.

Of the remaining three organizations, two have significant ties to government. The CCSD began as the Canadian Welfare Council, which was a middle-class nongovernmental organization concerned with social policy. Its board of governors was composed of a cross-section of business, academic, and governmental elites, and most of its active members were professionals engaged in the welfare field. As a consequence, the organization was seen as a captive of state interests (Haddow 1990, 216-17). In the 1970s, the organization became the CCSD and changed its mandate to focus on research, most of it funded by the federal government. The NCW was created by the federal government in 1970 to advise the minister of national health and welfare. It relied entirely on the federal government for funding and its membership was predominantly middle class (Haddow 1990). The only group of these three that is an organization of the poor was NAPO, founded in

1971. Since its inception, it has relied heavily on federal government funding. Haddow (1990, 230) reports that "NAPO saw representing the poor as its main priority. In recent years its membership has grown significantly to include, in 1989, about 1,000 individuals and 150 organizations. Most individual members were middle class, but NAPO's executive bodies were largely filled by the approximately one-fifth of its members who have had some experience of poverty. Most staff members also had a poverty background." In short, "NAPO could not claim to have mobilized more than a small fraction of Canada's poor people" (ibid.). Thus only one national organization has been able to mobilize people living in poverty, and even that organization has not been able to mobilize large numbers of citizens.

A wide range of antipoverty organizations exists at the local level; many of these groups provide services for clients as well as acting as advocates. Although there are no comprehensive studies of these organizations, one study of activism in northern Ontario concluded that the most prominent antipoverty organization there "likely could not exist without government support" (Vickers 1998). This highlights the significance of government funding for the mobilization and maintenance of organizations representing Canadians with limited material resources.

A highly visible antipoverty organization that does not receive government funding is the Ontario Coalition Against Poverty (OCAP), which was formed in 1990 with the purpose of "mobilizing poor and homeless people to fight back through militant, direct action" (OCAP 2002, 2). The organization has played a prominent role in organizing demonstrations against the Ontario government, particularly following the election of a Conservative government in 1995. OCAP has also employed a tactic it calls "Direct Action Casework," which involves actions such as picketing agencies and employers introducing workfare, taking over empty buildings to provide shelter for the homeless, and resisting the closing of rooming houses in poor neighbourhoods (OCAP 2002, 3-4). It is not clear whether the organizers of OCAP are in fact poor people, or whether they are a self-styled "vanguard" determined to mobilize the poor. Certainly, the organization's language of "mobilizing" the homeless and "leading them" in protests suggests the latter.

Antipoverty groups are not alone in requiring significant state sponsorship in order to mobilize. Other marginalized groups such as the disabled, women, or ethnic groups have tended to rely heavily on funding from the federal government both for their initial mobilization and their ongoing operation. For instance, in the disability sector,

Boyce et al. (2001, 58-9) note that disability groups organized by parents of the disabled that welcomed medical professionals tend to be funded by the public out of a sense of charity, while groups composed of disabled people focusing on human rights tend to have trouble raising money. As a consequence, these latter groups have turned to government for support. In Canada, the obstacles to group mobilization posed by Olson's free rider problem and the unequal distribution of resources within society have to some extent been overcome through state intervention.

The Role of Government

The federal government's extensive role in providing funding to advocacy groups can be traced to 1970. The central agenda of the federal government at the time was the pursuit of Pierre Trudeau's vision of a "just society," which entailed both social justice and participatory democracy. In this context, the Department of the Secretary of State "had a clear mandate to mobilize Canadian society on the linguistic and broader participatory front ... The mandate referred vaguely to the disadvantaged, which clearly included the core constituencies that the branch had cultivated and connected with over the years: immigrants, Natives, youth and, most recently, official-language communities. But it could embrace the elderly, women and virtually any group or organization struggling to participate in the political process for the first time or against what then was referred to as 'the establishment'" (Pal 1993, 109-10). For the next three years, the federal government vastly increased its funding of these groups, resulting in what one observer called the "great Ottawa grant boom" (ibid.) during this period. At the same time and through the same impulse, the federal government also began funding consumers' organizations through the newly formed Department of Consumer and Corporate Affairs.

Pross (1992, 71) argues that in the late 1960s and early 1970s, federal government departments were sponsoring the formation of advocacy groups in order to bolster the departments' fight for power with the central agencies of government, most notably the Privy Council office. He notes that "a great many latent and solidary groups – like the independent fishermen of Canada's east coast – found themselves exhorted to organize themselves into interest associations. For those who could not afford to organize themselves in this way, agencies provided financial incentives ... In these various ways federal agencies have sought to develop interest communities capable not only of creating a link with a specific clientele or sector constituency, but also of supporting each agency and its policies in the turbulent policy process that currently prevails." Government departments sponsor the formation of groups not only to strengthen their position vis-à-vis other government agencies but also to create allies in public debates over policy issues.

During the Trudeau era, funding of advocacy groups became established practice within the federal government, particularly in the departments of the Secretary of State, Consumer and Corporate Affairs, and Health and Welfare. Pal (1993, 246) reports that by the mid-1980s, the Secretary of State was funding 3,500 organizations, mainly official-language minority groups, multicultural organizations, and women's groups. Many of these organizations were small, local, service-oriented groups, but national political advocacy groups were also funded.

The full extent of government funding of advocacy groups is virtually impossible to gauge. One study commissioned for the Department of Consumer and Corporate Affairs tried to estimate total expenditures made by federal government departments and agencies to advocacy groups. The authors reported that the estimates "met with a great deal of criticism from officials in some departments who claimed that the information was inaccurate and incomplete" (Finkle et al. 1994, 131 n. 270). The authors' unpublished estimate was for the 1986-7 fiscal year; after excluding payments to groups for services that had nothing to do with policy advocacy, they calculated that seventeen federal departments had paid almost $185 million to over 500 groups (Pross 1992, 205). Of these funds, six bilingualism-related groups received over $1.6 million, six consumer groups received a total of $1.7 million, sixteen environmental groups received $2.1 million, forty-six health-related groups received $5.6 million, and twenty-three legal/human relations groups received $4.5 million (Pross 1992, 300 n. 48). Although the federal government has traditionally been the largest player in funding groups, provincial and municipal governments are also involved. Again, no estimate is available of the extent to which these governments fund advocacy groups.

However, state support for advocacy groups has clearly declined over the past decade. Susan Phillips (1995, 2-3) notes that "the Mulroney government began selectively cutting grants and contributions to groups in 1986-7. Almost every budget since has announced new and significant across the board cuts." In 1992 there were cuts of 20 percent over two years, and the 1993 budget deepened these by 15 percent. Continuing the policy, the Chrétien government undertook selective cuts specifically targeting advocacy and public education groups (ibid.).

In addition to decreasing the funding made available to groups, the federal government has pursued a policy of offering only program funding, rather than core funding. This means that groups can apply for funds to undertake a specific project, but not to cover ongoing costs like staff salaries or rent for office space. As a result, groups have had to look to other sources for their ongoing funding. A survey of 200 key informants, most of whom were the top executives of civil society organizations, found that the majority of respondents believed that "some" or "many" civil society organizations had had to terminate their operations due to lack of funding during the previous year (Embuldeniya 2001, 14). Nevertheless, this change in government practice has not necessarily been fatal to groups. A study of eight nonprofit organizations between 1993 and 1998 found that of the eight, six had increased their government funding over the period studied. The form in which this funding was obtained changed, as long-term program support was reduced or eliminated and funds were delivered through short-term project support. These changes did not impair the ability of these organizations to engage in advocacy activities (Juillet et al. 2001).

Federal government funding has had several consequences for the groups themselves. First and foremost, as we have seen, government funding facilitated the mobilization of groups that otherwise might not have been able to organize; it has allowed groups that otherwise might not have had a voice to participate in the policy process. In a country with a relatively small population geographically dispersed across a vast landmass, and with two official languages and considerable cultural diversity, the costs of mobilizing a national group are often prohibitively high. Government has stepped in to subsidize some of these costs, thereby increasing the extent and the diversity of the advocacy group system.

The second effect of government funding builds on the first: funding allows government to play a role in determining which marginalized interests will be able to mobilize and which will not. For example, the women's movement that began to appear in the early 1970s received much more government funding than did the gay liberation movement that was emerging at much the same time. As a consequence, the women's movement has mobilized more extensively at the national level and encompasses a much greater diversity of groups than does the contemporary gay rights movement. In making determinations regarding which groups will be funded, government pursues its own objectives. It is no coincidence that the federal government, preoccupied with considerations of national unity and pursuing its policy of official bilingualism, has provided extensive funding to official-language minority groups, some of which represent very small pockets of francophones in English-speaking Canada (see Pal 1993). Often, in order to receive funding groups must adhere to the core mission of the funding program: antibilingualism groups could not receive funding from the secretary of state, and nor could antifeminist groups receive funding from the secretary of state's women's program, which was committed to pursuing women's equality. The one exception to this was a grant given to the antifeminist organization REAL (Realistic, Equal, Active, for Life) Women by the Mulroney government. In these ways, governments can use funding to determine which interests mobilize the most successfully and in what form. In some instances, governments can privilege one perspective and virtually silence another. This is a deeply troubling aspect of reliance on state funding for advocacy groups.

Third, because the federal government has been most extensively involved in funding groups, groups have tended to focus on engaging with the federal government rather than provincial governments. This is not an absolute: in fact, some groups report using federal government funds to lobby provincial governments (Boyce et al. 2001, 131). This focus on the federal government is not an unintended consequence of its policies; in fact, substantial evidence suggests that a large part of the federal government's motivation in funding groups was to further its national unity agenda by encouraging the formation of national groups with a focus on the federal government (Pal 1993).

Fourth, government funding can affect the tactics a group employs. For example, groups representing gays and lesbians have not been given core funding from government, but have been able to access some funds under the Court Challenges Program, which subsidizes the cost of challenging the legality of laws under the Canadian Charter of Rights and Freedoms. This has had the effect of encouraging gay rights groups to use litigation as a strategy for political change (Smith 1999, 89). Receiving government funding may also encourage a group to favour mainstream tactics over more radical or "outsider" types of actions. For instance, one disability activist complained that once his organization started to accept government funding, they "started to slide into the abyss of back-room meetings ... [the group] became more co-opted, almost totally, by the bureaucracies in Ottawa" (in Boyce et al.

2001, 59). The potential for government to direct a group becomes much greater when only project funding – as opposed to core funding – is provided. Project funding forces groups to develop proposals that relate to the government's policy objectives rather than the objectives identified by the group's members and leadership.

Fifth, accepting government funding can affect the relationship between a group's members and its leadership. On one hand, the group may be compromised in the eyes of its members or supporters, who come to believe that the group's leadership has been co-opted by its relationship to government funding agencies. On the other hand, without government funding an organization can have difficulty maintaining adequate communication between its grassroots and leadership, thereby neglecting questions of internal democracy and accountability. For instance, Smith (1999, 148) reports that "lack of stable funding allowed a middle-class, white, mainly male, group to monopolize EGALE's leadership and political direction." Noting this phenomenon, Phillips and Orsini (2002) have argued that government contracts with voluntary sector groups should build in funding for internal capacity-building so that the group's leadership can remain responsive to its members.

Sixth, heavy reliance on government funding can leave groups vulnerable to sudden changes in this funding. Government funding makes it less necessary for groups to develop extensive donor bases and to solicit other sources of financing. When government funding is withdrawn, groups are usually thrown into crisis. Raising funds through private donations can be a difficult task for some groups. The Canadian Centre for Philanthropy estimates that for every 1 percent cut in government grants to charities, a 5.8 percent increase in individual donations and a 49 percent increase in corporate donations is needed to maintain the status quo (in Phillips 1995, 2-3). Despite this, as government funding has declined over the past decade, many groups have been able to cope. Boyce et al. (2001, 131) note that when government funds were withdrawn, some disability organizations were able to find resources from other community groups, unions, and churches. This allowed their staffs and budgets to grow and increased the influence of the organizations. The labour movement has also stepped in to support many left-of-centre organizations when their funding from government was cut.

Clearly, government funding is not unproblematic. Groups struggle with the question of whether to seek government funds, and many – including such major national organizations as the Council of Canadians and the Canadian Taxpayers Federation – opt not to accept government funding in any form. Other groups see little choice but to solicit government funds to allow them to mobilize their supporters and act as public advocates. On the other side of the equation, the federal government has become increasingly unwilling to fund groups that will be critical of it, even though government officials may benefit from consultation with groups representing the interests and views of stakeholders in a particular policy field.

Arguably, the ideal situation in a democracy would be for groups to be funded entirely by their supporters. That way, a group's financial status would reflect its level of support among citizens. As we noted in Chapter 4, groups that rely on individual donors for financial support have an incentive to be responsive to the opinions of their supporters. Moreover, financial support from individual contributors can insulate groups from the detrimental effects of sharp declines in government funding. Despite our concerns about groups that encourage chequebook-only participation, we do acknowledge the importance of an independent financial base for the functioning of advocacy groups.

But to leave the funding of groups entirely in the hands of the market assumes that key resources, notably wealth, are equally distributed in society. Since this is not the case, we look to government to make some effort to even out inequities between various segments of society. Government also has a role to play in mitigating the effect of the free rider problem discussed earlier in this chapter. In recent years, the federal government has largely abdicated its role in correcting for these biases. As a consequence, diffuse interests and marginalized segments of society have been less well represented in the political sphere than they had been since the early 1970s.

Studies of the government's specific granting practices suggest that there is considerable room for improvement in how its grants are administered. First, administration should be transparent, with groups accountable for how funds are spent. In a more thorough discussion of these issues, Finkle et al. (1994) recommend that governments adopt a strict approach that would include prepublication of draft criteria for grants and processes for comment by affected parties, publication of the criteria for grants, procedures that allow groups to hear the case against their receiving funding and to respond to it, giving reasons for decisions, and regular publication of the names of groups that have received funding and for what purpose.

Second, the government's willingness to offer core funding to groups must not be tied to the group's perspective, but rather to a commitment to correct for inequities in resources and the dilemmas posed by the free rider problem. Although this would not be a simple task, it is worthy of some deliberation. One mechanism for achieving this would be to remove decisions regarding grants to advocacy groups from government departments. An arms-length government agency with an explicit mandate to provide core, multiyear funding to groups representing marginalized segments of society and diffuse interests would go a long way toward depoliticizing the process of funding these groups. Such an agency would need to operate according to the procedures that Finkle et al. (1994) set out for ensuring accountability and due process in decision making.

Third, if we want groups to be able to bring the perspectives of a wide range of segments of society into the formal political arena, then all levels of government need to make funding available to groups to participate in consultations, legislative hearings, or regulatory processes. This involves not only the travel costs associated with participating but also the costs entailed in consulting with group members to develop a policy stance, preparing a submission and, if necessary, hiring legal counsel for regulatory hearings. Once again, a distinction must be made between corporations or industry associations and citizens' groups. For the former, costs associated with lobbying government are the costs of doing business. The latter have no expectation of monetary gain, and may face prohibitive financial obstacles. In these instances, governments that want genuine consultations with interested parties must remove financial barriers.

The Taxation System

While direct government funding is important to some groups, the most significant way in which government affects the resources available to advocacy groups in general is through the taxation system. Most nonbusiness advocacy groups receive no benefits via the income tax system, although the organizations themselves are exempt from paying income taxes. Supporters of a group cannot claim a credit on their income tax when they make a financial contribution, unless the group enjoys charitable tax status. As discussed below, however, such status significantly curtails a group's ability to engage in advocacy activities.

In contrast, when a business engages in lobbying the government, the expenses incurred in this process (including hiring a paid lobbyist or paying membership fees in an industry association) are considered business expenses. If a business spends $500,000 lobbying government, this amount is claimed as a business expense and therefore reduces the amount of tax the corporation owes the government. This situation creates a clear imbalance between businesses and other groups lobbying government and, as one observer noted, has "the peculiar effect of encouraging the lobbying of government by commercial and private interests, and hindering lobbying by non-commercial entities that are often pursuing a broader public interest" (Bridge 2000, 16).

The only groups (aside from registered political parties) that can offer tax receipts to their contributors in Canada are registered charities. Charities also enjoy a number of other tax benefits, including exemption from federal income tax and the GST. In order to qualify as a charity, a group must be engaged in one of the four following pursuits: relief of poverty, advancement of education, advancement of religion, or other purposes beneficial to the community. In addition, the federal government's regulations surrounding charitable status specify that a group cannot devote more than 10 percent of "the financial and physical assets of the charity as well as the services provided by its human resources" on advocacy activities (Bridge 2000, 4). Therefore groups dedicated primarily to advocacy cannot qualify for charitable status, and even groups that predominantly provide services must be very cautious in acting as advocates. The government modified this rule slightly in 2003, such that charities with annual income below $50,000 can devote 20 percent of their activity to advocacy, those with annual income below $100,000 can devote 15 percent, and all remaining charities can devote 10 percent of their activity to advocacy. Even with this modification, organizations like food banks must be careful not create a perception that they are lobbying government to increase welfare benefits because they risk losing their charitable status. Without this status, the group's ability to raise funds is much diminished. This places organizations in a difficult situation, particularly because there is a sense that the federal government "applies these ill-defined advocacy rules in an inconsistent, arbitrary or discriminatory manner. These perceptions, whether justified or not, exacerbate the confusion and create tension and distrust" (Bridge 2000, 14).

In light of these difficulties, a number of reforms have been suggested. Many of these recommendations focus on clarifying the advocacy activities that can be undertaken, and increasing the proportion of the group's activities that can be directed toward advocacy (see, for example, Bridge 2000). While these proposals have considerable merit, they maintain the distinction between charitable organizations like food banks, and nonprofit advocacy groups like environmental lobby organizations. Instead, perhaps advocacy groups should be given the same tax benefits as charities. Three arguments can be offered in favour of such a policy change.

First, advocacy groups make an important contribution to the political life of the country, both by providing information to political decision makers and by articulating the interests and opinions of segments of the Canadian population. This public service should be encouraged by the state. Indeed, the other intermediary organizations in Canadian politics – political parties – benefit from a tax credit that is more generous than the tax credit offered for charitable donations (see Carty, Cross, and Young 2000, ch. 7). The political contribution tax credit recognizes the significant role that parties play in contributing to Canadian democracy; why should advocacy groups not receive similar recognition?

Second, experience with the tax credit offered to contributors to political parties suggests that the existence of a tax credit encourages a larger number of citizens to make relatively small contributions to parties. Presumably, the same incentive would work for advocacy groups. This would make groups' fundraising efforts more successful, thereby strengthening their internal capacity and reducing their reliance on direct support from government.

Third, by encouraging small contributions from individuals, the tax credit would at least partially avoid the difficulties inherent in governments providing grants directly to groups. Such a system would allow citizens to determine to which groups they want their tax dollars directed, rather than allowing the state a monopoly on this decision. Groups able to appeal to a broad range of citizens would be able to raise more funds than those with more limited appeal. Government would have a role in remedying inequities stemming from uneven distribution of resources and overcoming the free rider problem, but these inequities could be lessened by giving groups an important tool that allows them to solicit contributions more easily.

Such a reform would, of course, entail developing rules regarding what groups qualify as registered public interest associations. In the case of political parties, achieving registered party status is a prerequisite for having access to the tax credit. In the past, parties have had to nominate fifty candidates in an election in order to achieve or maintain this status. This requirement was struck down by a Supreme Court ruling, and in 2003 the government introduced legislation that would allow parties to register even if they ran only one candidate and collected the signatures of 250 party members. To gain charitable status, an organization must meet stringent tests that its activities and purposes provide a tangible benefit to the public and that its purposes are charitable (see CCRA 2003).

The system for registering charities could be used as a basic model for granting advocacy groups charitable tax status (see also Pross and Webb 2002). In addition, the Voluntary Sector Initiative's Joint Table report offers some restrictions that warrant consideration: it suggests that political activities should contribute to the organization's stated objectives, and that political activities be nonpartisan, not involve illegal speech or illegal acts, be within the powers of the directors of the organization, not be based on information that the group knows or ought to know is inaccurate or misleading, and be based on fact and reasoned argument (cited in Bridge 2000, 24). Aside from the last criterion, which seems designed to invite arbitrary government decisions, these are reasonable restrictions to place on a group that wishes to benefit from public funds (in the form of taxation revenue foregone by the government).

Evaluating Which Interests and Identities Are Mobilized

In this chapter, we have seen that both the free rider problem and inequitable distribution of resources in society can hinder the mobilization of certain kinds of advocacy groups. In Canada, these hindrances have frequently been overcome through government funding. In recent years, however, government funding has decreased and has taken forms that make it more difficult for groups to mobilize, and to develop or maintain their internal capacity. This has made it more difficult for marginal voices to be heard in the policy process. However, there is a significant role for government to play in overcoming these obstacles to mobilization. We advocate core funding to groups facing these obstacles, as well as strengthening advocacy groups' capacity to raise funds from the public by extending them taxation status equivalent to that enjoyed by charitable organizations.

Chapter 5

Strengths

- In some instances, groups representing marginalized or diffuse interests have been able to mobilize, particularly with the assistance of government funds.

Weaknesses

- Government support for groups has declined precipitously in the past decade, making it more difficult for marginalized and diffuse interests to mobilize effectively.

- The taxation structure governing businesses and nonprofit groups is inequitable, favouring business groups over other advocacy organizations.

- The tax system does nothing to encourage the formation or development of advocacy groups but does a great deal to help fund political parties.

TALKING TO GOVERNMENTS 6

In the previous chapter, we saw that certain kinds of interests and segments of society find it more difficult to form advocacy groups than do others, creating inequities in the advocacy group system. In this chapter and Chapter 7, we turn our attention to the potential consequences of these disparities, asking which groups are heard in the public policy process. We also examine the ways in which groups make their voices heard, focusing on the tactics they employ and the consequences of these tactics both for a group's ability to achieve its objectives and for Canadian democracy as a whole.

Two of the Audit criteria are relevant to this discussion. As in the previous chapter, inclusiveness is at issue. Do groups representing marginalized segments of society face particular obstacles to making their voices heard within the policy process? Is there evidence of persistent bias in favour of well-resourced groups, particularly those representing business? If this is the case, then the policy process is neither as inclusive nor as equitable as the democratic ideal would demand. Related to this is the issue of responsiveness. How open are Canadian governments to consulting with advocacy groups? Do Canadian governments tend to favour certain sets of interests, or do they hear from a wide range of stakeholders in the course of developing public policy?

Our discussion will focus on five sets of strategies employed by groups. This chapter examines the two most common forms of direct contact between groups and governments: lobbying of decision makers and participation in formalized government or legislative consultation

processes. Chapter 7 discusses other forms of activity by which advocacy groups try to influence public policy, specifically litigation,
involvement in elections, and protest activities. Many groups, particularly social movement organizations, place great emphasis on influencing the views of their fellow citizens. To some extent, this is
accomplished through the strategies listed above, but many organizations also devote considerable resources to directly convincing other
Canadians of the justice of their cause. While recognizing this tactic as
highly significant, we will not discuss it in any detail because it does
not involve engagement with the state.

In particular, for each strategy we will ask the following questions:

♣ What types of groups tend to employ this strategy, and why?
♣ For which groups does this strategy work best?
♣ How effective does this strategy tend to be?
♣ Does this practice contribute to or detract from the vitality of
Canadian democracy?
♣ Is regulation or state organization of this practice adequate?

These questions allow us to assess the overall impact of advocacy
group activity on the Canadian political system.

Lobbying

The term "lobbying" refers to the practice of communicating, usually
privately, with government officials to try to influence a government
decision. Meetings are initiated by the lobby group, not the government. Although the term "lobbying" usually conjures up images of
Gucci-clad paid lobbyists trading on their political connections to gain
access for their clients, our definition also encompasses informal contacts and grassroots lobbying by volunteers.

Informal encounters with decision makers require access, and are
therefore easier for group representatives who travel in their social circles. For instance, Tom d'Aquino, president of the Council of Chief
Executives (formerly the Business Council on National Issues) reports
bumping into newly elected prime minister Brian Mulroney in 1984
and advocating free trade with the United States, a policy the Mulroney
government later adopted (Newman 1998, 156-7). This meeting was

possible because both of them lived in the same upscale Ottawa neighbourhood and had an established social relationship.

Those individuals who do not travel in the right social circles can purchase access to cabinet ministers and even the prime minister; contributions to special party fundraising events allow a limited number of donors to share a social occasion with a politician. Until corporate contributions to federal political parties were banned in 2004, businesses were major contributors to parties, particularly the party in government (see Cross 2004). In addition, a few interest groups also made contributions to parties. For example, in 2001 the Canadian Association of Petroleum Producers gave over $16,000 to the governing Liberals, the Canadian Bankers Association contributed $13,000 (in addition to the hundreds of thousands given directly by its member banks), and the Canadian Drug Manufacturers' Association gave almost $12,000 (Laghi and Leblanc 2002). Corporate contributions to candidates and political parties remain legal in a number of provinces, including Ontario, British Columbia, and Alberta, as are corporate contributions to candidates for municipal office in many cities and towns.

Organizations with large budgets can also create opportunities to talk to politicians by offering them hospitality. In Alberta, for instance, groups representing chemical companies, accountants, educators, telecommunications companies, and other interests routinely host a Wednesday night "Diner's Club" for members of the legislative assembly to educate them on issues of concern to the group ("Receptions show" 2003). The costs associated with such gatherings are relatively minor for corporate interests but would prove prohibitive for many citizens' groups.

These kinds of informal contacts can therefore be very difficult for groups representing marginalized segments of society to achieve. Some groups can, however, be very determined in their pursuit of decision makers. For instance, one disability activist involved in the campaign to include disability rights in the Charter of Rights and Freedoms recalls following then minister of justice Jean Chrétien and other members of Parliament to the washroom during a break in parliamentary hearings: "We were accused of making some of the members dribble on their shoes at the stalls because we kept distracting them" (quoted in Boyce et al. 2001, 61). Such exceptions aside, informal lobbying is largely the purview of groups whose members have either wealth or high social status.

Many advocacy groups – particularly those with fewer financial resources but active membership bases – try to influence decision makers by organizing volunteer lobbies. These lobbies can involve coordinated visits by grassroots activists to legislators in their constituency offices, visits by group members to MPs' Ottawa offices, or lower-key programs of volunteer visits to legislators, officials, and ministers (Pross and Webb 2002, 13). In their study of twenty advocacy groups and charities involved in advocacy activities at the national level, Pross and Webb found that sixteen of the groups used grassroots lobbies, ten of them frequently.

While grassroots lobbies are organized by advocacy group leaders and rely on volunteer efforts, some groups hire a professional lobbyist to help them map out their lobby strategy and gain access to key decision makers. Businesses and industry associations are by far the biggest users of paid lobbyists. We are able to measure the extent of this because all paid lobbyists operating at the federal level are required to register and disclose information regarding their activities. Two types of lobbyists must register: consultant lobbyists, who are contractors hired to work on behalf of a company or group, and in-house lobbyists, who are employees of the company or group.

To estimate the extent to which business interests employ paid lobbyists, we analyzed the list of consultant and in-house lobbyists registered at the federal level as of July 2002. We analyzed the entire list of organizations with registered in-house lobbyists, and we drew a random sample of 60 percent of the clients of the consultant lobbyists. Categorization was in both cases based on the name of the group. Our figures may overestimate the dominance of business somewhat, as voluntary organizations are not required to register, and some nongovernmental organizations may be unaware of the registration requirements (see KPMG 2001). In July 2002 just over 90 percent of the clients of consultant lobbyists were corporations or industry associations. Of the noncorporate registrations, the majority were for other governments (municipal, provincial, and foreign), institutions such as universities, First Nations band councils, and unions. Only a very small number of nonprofit groups (including Greenpeace, Habitat for Humanity, and the Canadian Cancer Society) had hired lobbyists.

There were also 152 corporations and 355 organizations with registered in-house lobbyists. Of the 355 organizations, 76 percent were business or trade associations, professional associations, unions, or institutions. Less than one-quarter were nonprofit organizations, including both predominantly service-oriented groups, like the Red Cross and Canadian Cancer Society, and advocacy groups, like the National Action Committee on the Status of Women and the Animal

Alliance of Canada. From this analysis, it is evident that the vast majority of lobbying activity is intended to pursue selective, rather than collective, benefits. In particular, business is the most heavily engaged in lobbying activity.

Why is lobbying a tactic favoured by business interests? Lobbying by definition requires access to decision makers. Access is best attained when a group or interest is perceived by those decision makers to have a legitimate role in providing information or expressing opinions regarding matters of public policy. When it comes to the regulation of industry, business is almost inevitably accorded this legitimacy. As a consequence, businesses and business groups are often better able to gain access. Access is not guaranteed, however, so businesses hire consultant lobbyists in the hope that politically connected insiders can open doors on their behalf. Given that the fees charged by consultant lobbyists are not paltry, corporate interests are also much more likely than nonprofit organizations to be able to afford consultant lobbyists. Even if public-interest groups can afford to hire a lobbyist, some consider it inappropriate for a nonprofit group to do so. Pross and Webb (2002, 17) report that some of the leaders of nonprofit groups they interviewed would not hire lobbyists because "that is not what we are all about" and "we want representation from [our own] community."

How effective is lobbying? The large sums of money devoted to employing in-house government relations personnel and to hiring consultant lobbyists suggests that lobbying must yield some benefit, or at least that many senior corporate executives believe that lobbyists can help them. Paid lobbyists are considered to be effective because they have direct access to senior politicians, they have expertise in designing effective campaigns of persuasion, and they are able to get more accurate feedback on the effectiveness of lobbying efforts than can the average advocacy groups.

Nonetheless, many corporations do not perceive consultant lobbyists to be particularly effective. A survey of senior civil servants and executives of major corporations found that both the government and business respondents preferred to deal with in-house government relations representatives. Of the business executives surveyed, 64 percent indicated that they preferred to deal with in-house representatives, as did 58 percent of government respondents. Government respondents tended to rate industry associations more highly as representatives, with 71 percent of respondents preferring to deal with them, as compared to only 42 percent of business respondents. Among both sets of respondents, consultant lobbyists were the least popular of the three choices: only 17 percent of business and 11 percent of government respondents preferred to deal with them (PPF 2001, 17). (Percentages add up to more than 100 percent for each group because respondents could select more than one.)

When asked what activities were effective in influencing decision making, only 30 percent of business and 27 percent of government executives thought hiring consultant lobbyists was effective. Both groups ranked such activities as face-to-face meetings with politicians and public servants and maintaining coalitions of like-minded companies as more effective. However, both groups ranked all lobbying-type activities as being much more effective than such activities as presentations to House of Commons committees, contributions to political parties or candidates, direct mail campaigns, and paid advertising (PPF 2001, 18).

To the extent that business respondents found paid, consultant lobbyists helpful, it was in identifying government decision makers, providing strategic advice, assisting in making appointments with decision makers, and providing guidance on the factors underlying a government initiative. Notably, these were precisely the functions that the respondents found their trade and industry associations were poorly equipped to perform. Only one-quarter believed that paid lobbyists could effectively provide direct representation to government. Among government respondents, however, 38 percent thought lobbyists could provide direct representation (PPF 2001, 15). Evidently, lobbyists' ability to gain access to decision makers for their clients is significant.

What can we say about the practice of paid lobbying from an Audit perspective? The principle of free speech and the Audit value of participation together lead us to conclude that groups are entitled to lobby decision makers and to hire paid lobbyists to assist them in this activity. From the perspective of inclusiveness, however, lobbying is clearly a practice dominated by interests with greater financial resources. In this respect, access to government – or at least to advice about how best to approach government – is not equally available to all societal groups, but rather to those that can afford the fees of paid lobbyists.

The practice of lobbying also raises questions about political corruption. It takes place behind closed doors, so little is known about the agreements that emerge between advocacy groups and public decision makers. Moreover, paid lobbyists are sometimes accused of influence peddling. Most lobbyists have partisan political connections in Ottawa and may, on occasion, trade on them in order to gain information or access for a client. For instance, in the summer of 2002, Warren Kinsella was registered as a lobbyist on behalf of six corporate clients, including the mining company INCO, Labatt Breweries, and United Airlines. At the same time, he appeared frequently in the media as a staunch supporter of Prime Minister Jean Chrétien, who was at that time fighting off a challenge to his leadership of the Liberal Party. Similarly, Ottawa lobbyists were so heavily involved in the campaigns to elect a new Liberal leader in 2003 that one media account concluded that "[paid] lobbyists are much of the human elbow grease of this leadership race" (Curtis 2003). These volunteer efforts presumably guarantee lobbyists who backed the winning candidate access to the new prime minister. Such close personal relationships again lead us to the conclusion that lobbyists are not merely providing advice; they are using their partisan connections to open doors.

Such concerns provided the impetus to regulate lobbying at the federal level. In the early to mid-1980s, there was considerable unease regarding the growing government relations industry in Ottawa as insiders with Liberal contacts, and then in 1984 with Conservative connections, began to establish large and successful government relations firms (see Sawatsky 1987). In response to these concerns, the federal government introduced legislation establishing a Lobbyists Registry. The legislation required that both consultant lobbyists and in-house lobbyists for corporations and organizations register and provide information regarding their clients, the matters on which they are lobbying, and with which departments they are in contact. The intention of the legislation was to make the lobbying industry transparent, as the registry would make public which interests were lobbying government on what issues. In 1997 the federal government also adopted a Lobbyists' Code of Conduct, which requires that lobbyists disclose to public office holders on whose behalf they are making a representation, provide only accurate and factual information to office holders, not divulge confidential information, not represent conflicting interests without informed consent of the interests involved, and avoid placing public office holders in a conflict of interest by proposing or undertaking actions that would constitute improper influence. The Code of Conduct is administered by the federal ethics counsellor. Since the code was adopted in 1997, he has not found merit in any complaints made regarding alleged breaches of the code.

Although the Lobbyists Registry goes some distance toward making the practice of paid lobbying transparent, it suffers from a number of deficiencies. First, the information provided by lobbyists with respect to their purpose in lobbying can be extremely vague. It is entirely acceptable for a lobbyist to submit a registration listing numerous government departments that will be lobbied on behalf of a client, and to indicate only that he will be lobbying "to seek business opportunities for the client." More specific information regarding the type of contract or regulatory issue on which the client is lobbying would increase transparency markedly.

Second, there is evidence that compliance with the law is not complete. The Office of the Ethics Counsellor commissioned a study that involved interviewing consultant and in-house lobbyists to gain their perceptions of rates of compliance. The report found that "a minority of registered lobbyists thought there was or might be non-registered lobbying going on among peers in their category of lobbyist (50 percent of consultant, 20 percent of organization, and 15 percent of corporate lobbyists indicated awareness of non-registered lobbying)" (KPMG 2001, 1). When asked why their peers might not be complying with the law, the respondents suggested both that there was ignorance of the requirements of the law and that some individuals were consciously avoiding the requirements.

Noncompliance is related to the third problem with the legislation: it relies entirely on lobbyists to register, and provides no check to ensure that they do so. Public servants and politicians are under no requirement to ensure that the individuals they meet with are properly registered, nor are they required to report with whom they have met. Noncompliance can only be caught, then, when complaints are made. Since the legislation was adopted in 1987, no complaint has led to charges; this suggests that those who choose not to register have little to fear in the way of sanctions.

Periodic parliamentary review of the legislation has not yielded significant amendments; this is not surprising given that of sixteen submissions to the committee, three were from government, ten were from lobbyists or groups representing lobbyists, and only three were from nonlobbyist organizations. Of those three, one was a publishing company that sells its product, the *Lobby Monitor*, primarily to lobbyists. The only critical voice came from the group Democracy Watch, whose concerns were not taken seriously in the committee's final report.

In short, regulation of lobbying activities has provided only partial transparency at the federal level and has been limited by the prominent role of lobbyists themselves in shaping the legislation. Only four provinces have adopted legislation governing lobbyists, and their legisation shares the deficiencies of the federal legislation on which it was based. We return to the question of regulating lobbying in Chapter 9.

Government Consultations

While lobbying involves private meetings between interested parties and government, sometimes involving a paid intermediary, government consultations are private or public forums in which groups and citizens are given the opportunity to share their views with decision makers. While lobbying contacts are initiated by advocacy groups, government consultations are initiated by government. We include a wide range of activities under the rubric of public consultations, including legislative or parliamentary hearings, hearings held by royal commissions or government task forces, consultative processes set up by government departments to solicit input, and advisory committees that include representatives of relevant advocacy groups.

For governments, consultation processes are a way to collect policy-relevant information, involve groups, gauge the impact of policy decisions on particular groups, solicit input on proposals, and improve service to the public. Consultation processes may also be an opportunity to try to bring relevant groups onside by providing them with information, involving them in decision making, and in some cases seeking consensus among competing interests (Sterne and Zagon 1997, 9). Consultation lends legitimacy to government decisions, as officials can present policies or legislation as the product of extensive discussion with stakeholders.

For groups, the prime reason to participate in some form of consultation with government is to influence the policy outcome. Additional objectives may include enhancing the group's relationship with relevant policy makers, gaining recognition as an important player in a certain policy field, and increasing public support for the group's objectives by gaining publicity. Given the potential benefits for both government and groups, it is not surprising that the number of government consultation processes has multiplied at every level of government.

That said, engaging in government-sponsored consultation processes may not always serve the interests of a group. When groups believe that the outcome of consultations is predetermined, they may have little to gain by participating. Compounding this, their participation in the consultative process might lend legitimacy to a government decision that the group opposes. For instance, the Assembly of First

Nations decided not to participate in consultations held prior to the introduction of the First Nations Governance Act in 2002. They reasoned that the act was intended to extend a colonial relationship between First Nations and the federal government and preferred not to legitimize the legislation by participating in consultations. On one hand, the organization missed an opportunity to suggest changes to certain provisions of the legislation; on the other hand, the political costs of legitimizing legislation that the group saw as anathema to its members were too high.

Some groups may worry about the risk of co-option when they engage extensively in consultations with government. For instance, in an account of political organization among PEI potato farmers in response to the rise of a potato disease, Fullerton (1995) argues that an emerging protest movement among farmers was stopped when their representatives were invited to sit on a joint committee of the government. By forming the committee, Agriculture Canada was able to control the flow of information and stifle negative press coverage. As a result, argues Fullerton, potato growers ceded control over their situation to the government. Had the farmers opted not to back the committee process, they might have continued their protest activities and ultimately achieved greater influence over policy outcomes. In a similar critique of governments' use of consultations, a former vice-president of the Alberta Wilderness Association argues that the Alberta government "uses lengthy consultations to buy time while buoying the hopes and sucking the energy out of activists" (in Falconer 2001, 128).

Of the five group strategies that we are examining, consultative processes involve the widest range of participants. Few groups, whether they are national industry associations or small local advocacy groups, will pass up the opportunity to provide advice to government, whether it be through meetings with officials, presentations to parliamentary committees, or membership in advisory bodies. In their study of twenty national organizations involved in public-interest advocacy, Pross and Webb (2002) found that all of the groups had made presentations to parliamentary committees, fourteen consulted frequently with officials in one or more government departments, and ten sat on governmental advisory boards.

Although a wide range of groups engage in government consultations, a number of barriers can stand in the way of this kind of activity. At the most basic level, the barriers can be physical. When the federal government held hearings on the Charlottetown Accord, disabled activists reported that the rooms where the hearings were held lacked ramps for wheelchairs or were located on the second story of buildings without elevators. Another significant obstacle is financial: substantial costs are involved in travelling to a capital city to attend legislative hearings or other meetings. These costs matter little to well-resourced groups, but can be prohibitive for groups with little funding. For example, in her account of the campaign to introduce gun control legislation, Heidi Rathjen describes taking buses back and forth between Montreal and Ottawa, sharing hotel rooms with other activists, and being barely able to scrape together airfare to attend meetings in western Canada (Rathjen and Montpetit 1999).

A less tangible, but equally significant, barrier is the group's acceptability to government officials. In open forums, like legislative hearings, any group can request a hearing and most are heard. In other consultative forums, however, government officials have the power to determine which groups are legitimate members of the policy community on a given issue. These determinations are necessary from the perspective of government, as they keep the number of players and range of interests manageable and focused, but nonetheless act as a barrier to "outsider" groups.

To what extent do these sorts of barriers affect the inclusiveness of government consultations? In an effort to answer this question, we examined the list of groups testifying before three parliamentary committees looking at various policy issues between 1999 and 2001. It should be noted that counting the numbers of groups falling into various categories only gives us part of the picture regarding how well interests are represented in such forums; the quality of representation and how representations are received are also highly significant. Nonetheless, this technique gives us at least a superficial understanding of how inclusive the system of group representation is for parliamentary committees.

Six groups testified before a House committee studying refugee policy. Of these six, two were professional associations (the Canadian Bar Association and an association representing Quebec immigration lawyers), two were industry associations (representing the air transport and shipping industries), and two represented the interests of refugees. The last two groups were coalitions: the Canadian Council for Refugees encompasses approximately 140 organizations, and the Inter-Church Committee for Refugees represents twelve national church groups. In this instance, the three relevant interests were equally represented, at least in numeric terms. That said, one might argue that refugees' interest in refugee policy is more intense than lawyers' or transportation companies' interest in the subject, and therefore required more extensive representation.

A joint House-Senate committee studying child custody and access heard predominantly from groups representing women/mothers and men/fathers – each of these categories accounted for over 30 percent of the 123 briefs presented. The interests of the group most directly affected by child custody arrangements – children – were represented by only 6 percent of the groups making presentations to the committee. Groups representing grandparents' interests were represented to the same extent, while professional associations had greater representation (11 percent of all groups). In this instance, there is a clear imbalance in who was being heard. That there were few voices speaking on behalf of children is not surprising, given the very limited resources children have at their disposal to make themselves heard in complex government hearings.

The House of Commons Standing Committee on Foreign Affairs and International Trade held extensive hearings across the country regarding a proposed Free Trade Agreement of the Americas. Of the 158 groups that testified before those hearings, the largest segment – 47 percent – represented business or agricultural interests. Citizen groups accounted for 31 percent of the groups testifying. Unions made up 13 percent and research institutes the remaining 9 percent. While these numbers demonstrate a slight imbalance in favour of business interests, citizens' groups were also reasonably well represented. In this instance, the scope of the groups consulted appears reasonably equitable and inclusive.

From these three short case studies, there seems to be a reasonable degree of inclusiveness in the groups that appear before House of Commons committees. This is, at least in part, a product of the procedural openness of these committees – their multipartisan character makes them more inclined to hear from representatives of a wide range of groups. For this reason we are dismayed by the growing tendency of some Canadian governments to forgo legislative committees in favour of task forces comprised only of legislators from the governing party. This practice has long been in use in Alberta, and as David Docherty (2004) notes, has become much more common in the Ontario legislature and federal House of Commons in recent years.

In general, government consultation processes vary in their degree of inclusiveness. Sometimes the department organizing the consultation goes out of its way to ensure that all relevant interests gain representation; in other instances, little or no effort is made. For example, the group Democracy Watch alleges that during the one-year period (April 1995 to July 1996) when the secretary of state for international financial institutions was consulting with groups regarding proposed changes to the Bank Act, the minister held forty-five meetings with industry representatives and gave nine speeches to industry associations, but did not meet with a single consumer group (Democracy Watch 1997). This critical perspective is echoed by a survey of key informants, mainly top executives of civil society organization, that found that the majority of those surveyed believe that Canadian governments have not put in place appropriate mechanisms and channels to give civil society organizations access to government departments and agencies (68 percent), or to political representatives (78 percent) (Embuldeniya 2001, vii). The perception that government does not consult sufficiently is not restricted to nonprofit groups, however. A survey of executives of corporations found that only 18 percent agreed that "government consults on a regular basis with corporations before making decisions that affect industry," and only 23 percent agreed that "industry is consulted by government in the development of legislation." Public servants did not share this view, however. Fifty-four percent maintained that government consults on a regular basis, and 61 percent thought that industry was consulted in the development of legislation (PPF 2001, 5).

In part, this difference of perception may be a function of the vastly different perspectives advocacy groups and government officials have when it comes to consultation processes. Groups are seeking specific policy outcomes, while government officials are balancing a number of competing pressures. Canadian governments have become more extensively involved in consultation processes in recent years in an effort to increase the legitimacy of public policy development and outcomes in the public eye. In some cases, consultations have allowed groups to exercise substantial influence over policy outcomes. For example, in the early 1990s then justice minister Kim Campbell consulted extensively with women's organizations when drawing up "no-means-no" legislation governing sexual assault, giving these groups an opportunity to engage meaningfully in policy development. In other cases, governments have engaged in consultation processes with no intention of allowing them to affect policy outcomes. In his account of Health Canada's consultations with stakeholders regarding legislation to regulate assisted reproductive technologies (ARTs), Montpetit (2003a, 107) concludes that "Health Canada officials, knowing where they wanted to take the ART issue, were not interested in hearing ideas that would challenge their own." These officials held meetings of up to forty stakeholder groups at a time, making lengthy presentations about the content of the government's legislation and allowing only limited opportunities for groups to respond.

Just as there is considerable variation in the inclusiveness of various government consultation mechanisms, there is equally great variation in the effectiveness of these consultations, from the perspectives of both the groups involved and the government body holding the consultations. Having surveyed the literature regarding government consultations, Evert Lindquist (1994, 105-7) lists several prerequisites for effective consultations:

♣ Governments should consult only if there is an outstanding set of unresolved issues; otherwise participants will believe the consultations are symbolic.

♣ All participants should have a clear idea of the purpose of the exercise (e.g., to solicit information, to seek consensus among stakeholders, etc.).

♣ The consultation instrument should match the purpose of the exercise. For example, consensus among stakeholders might be reached more effectively through a private, as opposed to public, meeting.

♣ All groups that stand to be affected by an impending decision should have an opportunity to express their views.

♣ The agenda for the consultation must be realistic and organized to encourage productive discussions.

♣ Government should be somewhat accountable to those who participated in the exercise, for example by providing feedback to those who participated on how their advice was used in final decision making.

A key consideration in designing a consultative mechanism is its form. At one end of the spectrum are parliamentary or legislative hearings, and at the other are private meetings of various stakeholders, or groups that have an interest in a particular policy area. Each of these models has its merits and flaws. Legislative hearings are highly formalized public meetings during which groups present prepared briefs and then answer questions from legislators. Their public character allows groups to make their case for the record, as well as trying to influence the views of legislators. That said, legislative committees are rarely able to set the direction of government policy; more commonly they have influence only over the details of legislation. For a group that wants input on such details, legislative committees can be highly effective, but for groups that want to influence the intent of legislation, they are a less fruitful avenue. Stakeholder meetings behind closed doors generally do not aim to allow groups to make their case for the public record, but rather to try to establish consensus among relevant interests regarding policy. When groups have very different views, it can be difficult to develop any sort of agreement about the best way to proceed. In short, it is of considerable importance that policy makers design consultations in a form conducive to the particular set of actors and circumstances involved.

From an Audit perspective, then, it is rather challenging to draw conclusions about the extent to which government consultations with groups contribute to or detract from democracy. Despite the government's increasing use of consultative mechanisms, very little academic literature evaluates the success and impact of these consultative processes (a notable exception is Montpetit 2003a). To the extent that governments are consulting in good faith, before decisions are made, and are inclusive of the full range of politically relevant groups, consultations are an opportunity for groups to try to influence public policy. If these conditions are not met, then they are simply exercises in legitimization. Consultations that encourage stakeholders to reach consensus are particularly valuable, but may not be viable in all cases.

Evaluating Who Talks to Governments

Talking directly to government, whether by lobbying or participating in a government-led consultation process, lies at the heart of advocacy. These are the most direct, and often the most fruitful, ways in which advocacy groups can hope to influence the development and implementation of government policy. As we have seen in this chapter, these processes are less than ideally inclusive. Not only are groups with more money able to gain greater access by hiring consultant lobbyists, but groups deemed acceptable to government gain insider status and are invited into consultative processes while other groups must fight to make their voices heard.

These inequities demonstrate the importance of open access points to the policy-making machinery, preferably before policy has been developed. Forms of consultation like legislative committees and royal commissions, which are open to a wide range of participation and whose consultation processes are transparent, are of crucial importance, as they provide points of access to the political system for wealthy and poor groups, and for insiders and outsiders. Efforts to move away from these formalized, open processes toward less formal closed consultation processes detract both from inclusiveness and governments' capacity to be responsive to citizens.

Transparency is also important when it comes to letting citizens know which groups are paying for access to political decision makers. Legislation governing paid lobbyists should be improved at the federal level, and adopted in the provinces that lack it, so that citizens can find out with some degree of certainty which interests are intervening in this manner.

CHAPTER 6

Strengths

- ⚐ Requiring registration by lobbyists has increased transparency at the federal level and in several provinces.

- ⚐ There are extensive opportunities for groups to participate in government consultations. Many consultative processes are inclusive.

Weaknesses

- ⚐ Lobbying activities could still be more transparent, particularly in some provinces and at the municipal level.

- ⚐ Lobbying remains a means for groups with greater financial resources to gain access to decision makers, thereby working against the objective of inclusiveness.

- ⚐ Some government consultation processes are designed only to legitimize decisions already made, rather than consulting interested groups.

- ⚐ Groups in some instances lack the capacity and resources to participate effectively in consultation processes, thereby rendering such processes less inclusive.

- ⚐ The trend toward government party task forces replacing legislative committees to study policy options reduces groups' ability to be heard in the legislative arena.

7   ADVOCACY GROUP INVOLVEMENT IN ELECTIONS, LITIGATION, AND PROTESTS

We now turn our attention to the other three elements of advocacy group activity: election campaigning, litigation, and protests. Unlike lobbying and consulting with government, which involve direct contact with policy makers, these activities try to change public policy via other avenues. By involving themselves in election campaigns or engaging in protests, advocacy groups try to exert pressure on decision makers to alter policy. This largely takes the form of mobilizing public opinion. When they decide to go to court, advocacy groups are also trying to change policy, but in a more direct manner: by having a judge overturn the decision of elected officials. Litigation can also mobilize public opinion and raise a group's profile.

We will examine each of these three activities according to the criteria set out at the beginning of Chapter 6. When it comes to evaluating these activities from the perspective of democracy, we have to consider whether groups detract from the quality of representative democracy when they involve themselves in elections or go to court. Critics of advocacy groups assert that representative institutions, notably political parties and legislatures, are diminished when advocacy groups engage in nontraditional activities like advertising in election campaigns and challenging legislation before the courts. Our evaluation of advocacy groups' activities in these areas bears this criticism in mind.

Intervention in Elections

Elections are moments when the public's attention is more focused on politics than usual, and political parties may be more open to changing their platform in response to public pressure. Consequently some advocacy groups choose to intervene in the electoral arena. In their examination of advocacy group involvement in the 1997 general election, Carty, Cross, and Young (2000) found that groups involve themselves in election campaigns in three distinct ways. The first is to work on behalf of one party. This strategy is viable only when a group's membership is homogenous in its partisan leanings. For instance, in the 1997 election members of the National Firearms Association were so deeply opposed to the Liberal Party's gun-control legislation that the organization endorsed the Reform Party because of its vocal opposition to this policy. This did not cause controversy in the group, whose members tended to be supportive of Reform on other issues as well. When an advocacy group opts to endorse a party during an election, the group may be able to wield some influence if the party is elected. For groups that back losing parties, however, costs may be high in terms of lost access to government. Not surprisingly, then, groups that are already outside of established policy communities and with little access to government often endorse opposition parties. Already lacking influence, these groups have little to lose by taking a partisan position.

The second, and more common, strategy open to groups during elections is issue advocacy, whereby a group uses the opportunity presented by an election campaign to try to further its cause. Carty, Cross, and Young (2000) found that numerous instances of advocacy group involvement prompted reactions from parties in 1997. For instance, Friends of Canadian Broadcasting spent approximately $500,000 prior to and during the election in an effort to pressure the government to increase funding for the CBC. At a minimum, such activity allows a group to increase the profile of its policy concerns.

The third technique groups use during elections is to target individual MPs to try to punish them for their action or inaction on the group's issue. Carty, Cross, and Young (2000) found that several organizations targeted incumbents in the 1997 campaign. Most notable was the Canadian Police Association, which targeted nine Liberal incumbents who had opposed a private members' bill that would have prevented murderers sentenced to twenty-five years in prison from appealing for early release (the "faint hope" clause). The CPA's campaign involved billboards with photos of the targeted MPs next to pictures of convicted serial killers and murderers. In addition to these highly controversial advertisements, the nationalist Société Saint-Jean-Baptiste published an advertisement targeting Liberal incumbents for their party's belief that Quebec could be partitioned in the event of its separation.

The 1999 provincial election in Ontario was the site of one of the more extensive and well-publicized efforts to target incumbents and encourage voters to defeat them. This campaign was undertaken by an organization called the Ontario Election Network, which was comprised of a number of citizen groups and trade unions. The OEN's objective was to defeat the Conservative Harris government by encouraging strategic voting to overcome the split of the non-Conservative vote between the Liberals and the NDP. The OEN identified "swing" ridings, selected the Liberal or NDP candidate more likely to win, and then endorsed that candidate. In his account of the OEN's participation in the campaign, Brian Tanguay (2001) reports that the groups in the network poured "serious money" into the campaign, mainly in the form of employee time off to supply volunteers to targeted ridings. The OEN did not advertise its list of endorsed candidates, but rather worked to publicize each endorsement within the riding. The network also ran anti-Conservative television and radio ads provincewide. Analyzing the election outcome, Tanguay concludes that the OEN's campaign had a modest effect on the outcome of the election in the targeted ridings.

The 2000 federal election was the first in which individuals or groups were required to disclose election spending directly supporting or opposing a candidate or registered political party, including advertising that takes a position on an issue with which a registered party or candidate is associated. This disclosure permits a more comprehensive understanding of the extent to which advocacy groups participate in election campaigns and the character of this participation. However, this does not capture any advocacy group advertising that raised an issue without directly supporting or opposing a candidate or party.

Examining the disclosure reports of the thirty-nine "third parties" that advertised in the 2000 election, we find that advocacy groups were the most active category. Of the third-party groups, twenty-five appeared to be advocacy groups, six were individuals, five were unions, and three were businesses. (One was identified only as the "CDC" and could not be classified.) Of the twenty-five advocacy groups, six appeared to be fronts for businesses and municipal governments. More specifically, three of them – Victorians for a Strong Canada, Edmontonians for Anne McLellan, and Edmonton Supporters of Anne McLellan – had received only one contribution each. These contributions were from businesses, and the addresses for the group and its financial agent were both the same as that of the contributing business. One other group – the Coalition for Anne McLellan – received contributions from four companies, and listed the address of one of them in its contact information. Given that there is no evidence of individual involvement in any of these four groups, they are best classified as businesses despite their populist names. All four advertised only in one electoral district, either Victoria or Edmonton West, where incumbent cabinet ministers were facing tight races. Presumably, these third-party expenditures were intended to help the candidate in question circumvent the limits imposed on their expenditures in the electoral district. Two other groups – La coalition des citoyens contre les fusions municipales forcées and the Comité de citoyens de St-Augustin – received only one contribution each, in each case from a municipal government. It is impossible to determine from the disclosure reports whether there was citizen involvement in either of the groups.

The remaining nineteen advocacy groups that advertised in the 2000 election campaign represented a fairly diverse range of interests, from such industry associations as the Canadian Medical Association and the Canadian Trucking Alliance to groups with a single-issue focus, such as Canadians Against Bilingualism Injustice, the Campaign Life Coalition of Manitoba, and the Canadian Alliance of Student Associations (see Table 7.1). Groups with an interest in wildlife and environmental issues were particularly active in the campaign, especially in British Columbia. The International Fund for Animal Welfare advertised on radio in Vancouver and Victoria, the environmental group Wildcanada.net advertised in two Vancouver-area weekly newspapers, and the Animal Alliance advertised in Victoria and Edmonton. The BC Wildlife Federation, a group representing hunters and anglers, also advertised on radio in Vancouver-area ridings.

This brings us to the question of which kinds of interests are able to gain a voice via participation in election campaigns. One of the concerns that has driven efforts to regulate group spending during election campaigns is the ability of business interests to vastly outspend their opponents when they choose to intervene in election campaigns. This fear is not unfounded: in the 1988 federal election, which centred on the issue of whether Canada should enter into a free trade arrangement

Table 7.1

Twenty largest third-party advertisers, 2000 federal election

Group	Type	$ spent in ridings	$ spent nationally	Total spending ($)
Canadians against Bilingualism Injustice	Advocacy group	135,569	14,573	150,142
Canadian Medical Association	Advocacy group		62,722	62,722
Council of Canadians	Advocacy group		44,556	44,556
International Fund for Animal Welfare	Advocacy group		21,918	21,918
BCWF Political Action Alliance	Advocacy group	20,465		20,465
Canadian Alliance of Student Associations	Advocacy group		9,579	9,579
Canadian Trucking Alliance	Advocacy group		6,980	6,980
Wildcanada.net	Advocacy group	6,101	100	6,201
Animal Alliance	Advocacy group	5,985		5,985
Hon. John Wise and Friends	Advocacy group	5,383		5,383
CUPE BC Health	Union	5,079		5,079
Progressive Group for Independent Business	Advocacy group	1,421	3,589	5,010
Nova Scotia Federation of Labour	Union		4,949	4,949
Sporting Clubs of Niagara	Advocacy group	4,512	408	4,920
Campaign Life Coalition Manitoba	Advocacy group		4,773	4,773
Guy Desrosiers	Individual	4,701		4,701
Confédération syndicats nationaux	Union		4,522	4,522
TCA Local 1163	Union	3,224		3,224
Coalition contre fusion municipale	Advocacy group / Municipality	2,906		2,906
Victorians for a Strong Canada	Advocacy group/ Business	2,849		2,849

Source: Derived from reports filed with the Chief Electoral Officer of Canada, <www.elections.ca>.

with the United States, both business groups and anti-free-trade citizens' groups and unions were heavily involved in election advertising. Pro-free-trade forces spent a total of $3.6 million, while their opponents spent only $878,000 (Hiebert 1991, 22). This difference did not reflect public opinion on the issue, which was evenly divided. Rather, it manifested the greater financial resources available to business interests. The 1988 federal election was exceptional in focusing on a single issue and one in which corporate Canada had a great stake. In 2000, a more routine federal election lacking a central issue, our analysis showed business interests were almost entirely absent and citizen groups were the largest spenders. But under the right circumstances – if a particularly important economic issue were central to an election – we would expect business to outspend other interests on election advertising by a wide margin.

The effectiveness of election advertising by advocacy groups is a matter of considerable controversy. Statistical analysis of voting behaviour in the 1988 federal election could not find evidence of consistent effects from third-party advertising (Johnston et al. 1992, 163-4). In a study of the effects of group advertising in the 1997 federal election, Tanguay and Kay (1998) concentrated on two groups that targeted candidates in an effort to defeat them, concluding that the groups' efforts had little or no impact. In fact, of thirty-nine candidates targeted for defeat by the National Citizens Coalition, thirty-six improved their performances over the average for their party in that province.

This does not necessarily mean that intervening in elections is ineffective for groups. If their objective is to make parties – particularly governing parties – more receptive to their issues, they can be very successful. For example, Carty, Cross, and Young (2000) note that after a coalition of environmental groups placed a full-page advertisement in the *Globe and Mail* in 1997 concerning the government's failure to pass legislation protecting endangered species, the Liberal Party immediately posted a policy statement on its website outlining its position on the issue. Similarly, pressure from AIDS activists early in the 1997 campaign led the government to renew funding for AIDS research before election day (101).

From an Audit perspective, we perceive advocacy group involvement in election campaigns as generally contributing to the quality of democracy. Elections focus public attention on important political debates. While political parties have an important role to play in setting out alternatives for voters and organizing political competition, there is no reason to give them a monopoly over such debates during the election period. The issues that political parties have decided are of central importance to the campaign may exclude issues that are crucially important to segments of the public. If advocacy groups are not able to make their voices heard during these periods, these issues will not enter into the public debate. Significantly, in our analysis of advocacy group involvement in the 2000 federal election, few of the groups that advertised were interested in the campaign issues as defined by the major political parties. The issues raised by third-party advertising were endangered species legislation, official bilingualism, gun control, and funding for postsecondary education. None of these were issues that the political parties saw as centrally important. Perhaps voters did not see them as important either; the key point is that the freedom of advocacy groups to articulate these issues gave voters additional information when making their vote decision. This can only serve the best interests of democracy.

We are, however, concerned with the potentially corrosive effect of negative advertising and targeting candidates. Campaigns like the Canadian Police Association's 1997 effort to link incumbent members of Parliament with serial killers are distasteful personal attacks that add nothing to the quality of democratic deliberation. If such tactics were to become common in Canadian elections (as they have become in the United States), it would debase the level of debate. To date, most Canadian groups have held back from such attacks, and we encourage them to continue to articulate their political stances in constructive ways. That said, if tolerating negative campaigns is the price of allowing groups to raise issues other than those articulated by political parties, it is a price we are willing to pay.

The involvement of advocacy groups in election campaigns has prompted another criticism: many observers fear that advocacy groups compete with political parties as intermediaries between society and the state. In the context of election campaigns, the specific concern is that in the absence of controls on advocacy group spending, groups can "drown out" parties, which are limited in the amount they spend. From our analysis of group involvement in recent Canadian election campaigns, we conclude that groups do not threaten parties' ability to communicate policy alternatives effectively to voters during election campaigns. Some groups are working on behalf of one party, which cannot be seen to be taking away from parties generally. In most instances, groups raise issues the parties prefer not to discuss or do not consider important. This challenges parties to broaden the range of issues on which they take stances and to share with groups the ability to set the agenda of election campaigns. Even in 1988, the federal election in which advocacy groups were the most active, the $4.7 million spent by advocacy groups was only a fraction of the total spending by parties and candidates.

This brings us to the question of regulation of advocacy group spending in Canadian elections. The federal government and the governments of Quebec, British Columbia, and Manitoba have adopted legislation limiting the amount organizations other than registered political parties can spend during election campaigns, and requiring disclosure of the source of money spent on advertising during elections.

Since 1974 the federal government has adopted three different laws aimed at limiting third-party spending in election campaigns. Each of these three laws has been successfully challenged in court by the National Citizens Coalition. The same is true of legislation adopted by the government of British Columbia. The federal government's approaches began with an outright ban, moved to a $1,000 limit, and then to a $150,000 limit nationally and a $3,000 limit in each electoral district. In each instance, the Alberta courts have ruled that these limits infringe on Canadians' freedom of speech. In 2004, however, the Supreme Court of Canada ruled in *Harper v. Canada (A.G.)* that such limits are a justifiable limitation on freedom of speech as they support the objective of fairness in the overall electoral regime.

In our view, there is little danger that groups will drown out parties and candidates, particularly given the extensive public funding available to parties and candidates at the federal level with the changes to the Canada Elections Act passed in 2003 (see Cross 2004). It is essential to ensure that groups are able to articulate their views during moments when the electorate is focused on politics.

We do, however, believe that there is a compelling need for disclosure of the amounts groups spend and the sources of their donations. The public interest is served when we are able to track which groups are spending and in which ridings. In part, this lets us know whether individuals or organizations are trying to evade the spending limits for candidates and parties. When we see spending by groups like "Supporters of Candidate X" we have every reason to believe that spending limits are being evaded. Citizens are entitled to this information. Even more crucial is information regarding the source of funds for election advertising. It means very little when we see that an ad is paid for by "Citizens for Issue X." For voters to make informed judgments about the claims made in the advertisement, they need to know whether the sponsors of the ad were, in fact, citizens, or whether they were businesses with a pecuniary interest in the matter.

This information is particularly important now that corporations and unions cannot contribute to political parties. If they shift their efforts into the realm of third-party advertising, citizens must have relevant information to pass judgment on their claims. This requires not only the disclosure rules contained in the Canada Elections Act and provincial election laws in Quebec, British Columbia, and Manitoba, but also disclosure at the time ads are run. Disclosure prior to election day allows voters to evaluate information and, if they consider it appropriate, cast their vote accordingly. Pre-election disclosure is the approach taken in the United States, which demonstrates that such requirements are feasible.

Litigation

Over the past two decades, litigation has become a much more significant aspect of advocacy group activity in Canada. Groups are increasingly turning to the courts in an effort to achieve the policy outcomes
they desire. This judicial involvement can take a number of forms:
groups can challenge the constitutionality of laws under the Charter of
Rights and Freedoms, or when a Charter case has been launched by
others they can seek status as interveners in the case in an effort to
shape the outcome of the court's decision. An example of a group challenging the constitutionality of a law would be the National Citizens
Coalition's efforts to have the courts strike down legislation limiting
third-party advertising in elections, discussed above. Environment
Voters, another advocacy group that wanted to ensure that the legislation was struck down, was granted intervener status by the court and
also made a submission in the same case. Groups can also bring suits
against government to try to force an action, such as requiring an environmental impact assessment before a large dam is built.

The use of litigation as a means of achieving political change is a
relatively new phenomenon. In his study of Canadian groups' use of litigation, Hein (2000, 8) notes that until the 1980s, few organizations
representing either business or other interests entered the courtroom
to influence public policy. The most significant factor changing the
level of group involvement was the entrenchment in 1982 of the Canadian Charter of Rights and Freedoms. The Charter created unprece-
dented opportunities for advocacy groups to pursue political change
via the courts.

When we think about advocacy groups engaging in litigation, the
first examples that come to mind involve equality-seeking groups like
gays and lesbians, Aboriginals, and women. While these groups have
made considerable use of the courts to achieve some significant policy
changes, they are by no means the only groups using the courts. In
fact, in his study of interest group litigation between 1988 and 1998,
Hein (2000, 9) found a remarkable range of groups using the courts,
and concluded that they are largely the same players who have traditionally sought to influence governments. In fact, his study found that
corporate interests accounted for almost half the legal interventions
by groups in that ten-year period. Corporate interests accounted for
468 interventions, equality-seeking groups such as women's and
refugee organizations 80, Aboriginal groups 77, labour groups 58, civil
liberties groups 40, and new left groups including gay and lesbian

groups 37. These numbers suggest that business interests are the pre-dominant users of litigation. In an absolute sense this is true. As Hein notes, however, businesses and business groups in Canada vastly out-number other advocacy groups. He concludes that businesses are less prone to using litigation than are advocacy groups, which is certainly the case.

Nonbusiness Canadian advocacy groups are not all inclined toward using litigation. In fact, this is a strategy employed only by a relatively small minority of groups. In their survey of twenty nonprofit organiza-tions operating at the national level, Pross and Webb (2002, 17) found that only one of the groups they studied used litigation "often" and nine used it "sometimes." They note that "litigation has become a slightly more popular technique in the 10 years between our two sets of inter-views, but remains a tool used either by wealthy organizations or by groups which specialize in this technique for affecting policy." Simi-larly, Hein (1997, 126) surveyed feminist and environmental organiza-tions to determine whether their executive directors preferred litigation over lobbying as a means for achieving policy change. He found that 62 percent of groups were "moderately optimistic" about lit-igation as a strategy, indicating that they believed litigation should be grafted onto traditional strategies in their arsenal. Only 12 percent saw litigation as a "powerful instrument of reform." Another 26 percent characterized litigation as a risky and time-consuming process.

The effectiveness of litigation for advocacy groups is difficult to measure. Certainly, some groups have used litigation to achieve out-comes that would have been difficult, if not impossible, without the courts. Groups representing gays and lesbians, for instance, have made remarkable gains through litigation. It is difficult to imagine that Canadian legislators would have granted the protections from discrim-ination and the positive rights – like the right to same-sex marriage – that have been won through the courts in recent years. Yet not all groups have been as successful with the judiciary. Labour groups, for instance, have made relatively few gains through the courts.

The question of whether groups' use of the courts contributes to or detracts from democracy is one of the most heated debates in Can-adian political circles. At the core of this argument is the assertion that unelected, unaccountable judges are supplanting elected politi-cians as the makers of Canadian public policy. This debate is discussed in greater detail in Ian Greene's (2005) volume in this series, but one aspect is of particular importance for our audit of advocacy groups' involvement in Canadian democracy: their use of the courts.

Some observers, most notably Morton and Knopff (2000), argue that the entrenchment of the Charter has ushered in a "Charter revolution" whereby legislatures and executives are weakened by the expanding power of an activist judiciary. Although they hold judges culpable for this, even more responsible is "the Court Party." This is the term they apply to a certain set of advocacy groups that have used litigation as a strategy for change: national unity advocates (particularly official-language minority groups), civil libertarians, equality-seekers, social engineers, and postmaterialists. The three latter categories are largely overlapping, and include feminists, gay and lesbian rights groups, racial minority groups, and peace and environmental organizations. These groups constitute a "party," according to Morton and Knopff, because they are partisans of the courts. In other words, they share an interest in the "systematic, policy-oriented use of judicial power" (2000, 84). The Court Party is a source of worry for Morton and Knopff not only because it allegedly seeks to empower unelected judges at the expense of elected legislators. The Court Party is also, in their view, a social elite comprised largely of lawyers, academics, and other socially privileged groups and individuals trying to impose its world view on a reluctant majority. In addition, groups engaged in litigation begin to frame their claims in terms of absolute "rights" instead of negotiable demands.

We take issue with Morton and Knopff's assertions on two grounds. First, their assessment ignores the extensive use that other groups – notably business, but also social conservatives – make of the courts (see Hein 2000). Second, little evidence supports their claim that groups have decided to pursue litigation at the expense of other strategies. Chapter 6 and the first part of this chapter detail the extensive involvement of advocacy groups in lobbying officials and legislators, engaging in consultation processes, and intervening in elections. Moreover, the research we have cited in this chapter demonstrates the considerable skepticism of many advocacy groups regarding litigation. Overall, we concur with Hein's (2000, 25) conclusion that the ability of so many groups to advance their claims through the courts is an accomplishment that Canadians should celebrate.

Advocacy groups' access to the Canadian courts is facilitated by three factors. The first is the rules governing standing in Canadian courts. In a 1981 decision, the Supreme Court ruled that a person did not need to be directly affected by legislation in order to challenge its constitutionality. This has greatly enhanced the ability of advocacy groups to challenge legislation. The second factor is the Supreme

Court's openness to granting intervener status to groups that want to try to influence the outcome of a case. The third factor is the Court Challenges Program, under which the federal government funds groups seeking to challenge the constitutionality of legislation.

While the first two factors developed as a result of a growing culture of openness in the Canadian courts, the third factor is a consequence of government policy. The Court Challenges Program was first established in the late 1970s to provide financial support to legislative challenges that advanced language rights outlined in the Constitution. With the entrenchment of the Charter of Rights and Freedoms, it was expanded to include equality rights in the 1980s. The program was cancelled in 1992 by Brian Mulroney's Conservative government despite a broad public outcry, but was re-established shortly after the election of the Chrétien Liberal government in 1993. It now resides under the responsibility of the minister of heritage and provides over $2 million a year to support organizations seeking to advance language and equality rights. The program is a valuable resource to groups representing women, persons with disabilities, gays and lesbians, and various cultural and minority communities who might not have the resources to research and prepare expensive challenges to laws that infringe upon the rights that the Charter was designed to protect. As such the program is an important way for governments to enhance the inclusiveness of the legal system (See Greene 2005). Along with the relaxing of the rules of standing and the courts' willingness to grant intervener status, the Court Challenges Program has remarkably increased the accessibility of the courts to advocacy group litigation.

Protest

The final strategy advocacy groups employ to draw attention to their concerns is protest. Protest tactics were introduced into Canadian politics by a series of social movements including labour movements that engaged in protests such as the Winnipeg General Strike. More recently environmental, student, and women's groups have held demonstrations, sit-ins, and marches on Ottawa, among other activities. Recalling that we have limited our inquiry in this book to consideration of groups engaging with government to achieve policy change, protest tactics might seem to be outside our range. But in our view, protest tactics are generally aimed at policy change, even if it is policy change that governments are unlikely to make. In many instances, protesters are trying to create public awareness of an issue, thereby creating pressure on government for policy change. In this regard, we consider protest tactics to fall within our mandate.

Protest tactics – which include holding demonstrations, organizing boycotts, and sometimes breaking the law – are usually associated with groups that are oppositional in their worldview, are less institutionalized, and have fewer resources at their disposal. These tendencies are not absolutes, of course. Greenpeace is an oppositional group that employs many protest tactics, some of which are illegal, but which also hires a paid lobbyist to work on its behalf in Ottawa. And although industry associations seldom demonstrate in the streets, it can happen. In the winter of 2000, downtown Ottawa traffic was paralyzed by long-distance truckers who drove their rigs in the direction of Parliament Hill, honking their horns and tying up traffic to protest high fuel prices.

Even taking these sorts of exceptions into account, it is fair to say that protest tactics are employed most frequently by oppositional, outsider-type groups. There are a number of reasons for this. First, if groups are not able to gain access to policy discussions, protest is virtually the only route available to them. Groups that are not considered legitimate stakeholders by decision makers can gain credibility and, in some cases, access, by putting on a demonstration of extensive public support. Second, protests are often effective in gaining media attention. In the era of television news, a highly visible protest is more appealing to journalists than testimony at a legislative hearing. Media attention is highly important to groups, both as a way of getting their message out and thereby gaining public support, and as a means of capturing the attention of decision makers. Third, protests help mobilize supporters, by making people feel that they are part of a campaign and may make a direct difference to policy outcomes. As we have seen at recent international conferences, a culture of protest has emerged among antiglobalization activists with festival-like gatherings taking place alongside international leaders' meetings. This can only help groups recruit new supporters.

When discussing the effectiveness of protest tactics, we must keep in mind that protests are not intended solely to exercise direct influence over public policy. Protest leaders may judge an event a success if it brings out many supporters, thereby strengthening the organization, or if it receives extensive media coverage. Either of these outcomes would be seen as strengthening support for the organization's objectives in the long term.

Regardless, several examples illustrate the potential for protests of various sorts to produce desired policy outcomes. In their account of activism supporting greater funding for AIDS research and support, Lindquist and Rayside (1992, 333-4) note that a protest march held at a national AIDS conference in Ottawa in 1988, at which then minister of health Jake Epp was burned in effigy, led to an increase in the federal commitment to AIDS programs from $8 million per year to over $32 million per year. Similarly, accounts of the impact of environmentalists' blockades of old-growth rainforest in British Columbia through the 1990s suggest that the protesters were able to bring about significant changes to the province's forestry practices and increase the amount of protected rainforest (see Stanbury 2000; Cashore et al. 2001).

By the same token, many groups hold large protests that do not have any impact at all on public policy. The Alberta group Friends of Medicare has held numerous protests in front of the Alberta legislature, but has not been able to deter the provincial government from its plans to reshape medicare. During the height of the debate over firearms legislation, opponents of the legislation held a large rally on Parliament Hill. In the estimation of a leading supporter of the legislation, "The ten thousand protesters who came to the rally were a great help to our cause. According to the accounts of media commentators, they came off as rude, selfish, rowdy and, as a group, very, very scary" (Rathjen and Montpetit 1999, 166). The government went ahead and adopted the legislation the protesters had opposed. In general, protest tactics appear to be somewhat high-risk for groups: they can produce results, but they can also backfire and reduce government sympathy for a group's cause. As public opinion polling has become well established within government, protests may have less effect than in the past. Governments now have the tools at their disposal to gauge the extent of public support behind a protest, and are less likely to be swayed by protesters who have little support in the general population.

Pross and Webb (2002, 16-17) found that three of the twenty groups they studied demonstrated "often" and six "sometimes." Only two of the three frequent demonstrators considered the protests to be an effective lobbying technique. Pross and Webb also report that when they compared their results to a study of the same groups carried out in 1992-3, the rate of protest activity and confidence in the efficacy of protests had both dropped. They speculate that this development may "reflect general trends in the patterns of policy discourse. It may be that the public is less receptive to the messages conveyed by demonstrations than it was ten years ago. Alternatively, groups may have found that the internet is a more compelling vehicle for disseminating policy views and securing public reaction" (17).

This brings us to the thorny question of whether political protest contributes to or detracts from the quality of democracy in Canada. Within certain limitations, protesters are exercising their rights to free speech and association, which are deserving of respect by the state and others. Indeed, as we noted in Chapter 3, support for the idea of political protest is very high among all Canadians, not just advocacy group activists. Beyond this, it is evident that protest is a means of rallying citizens to political action. The citizens who are mobilized in this way are, for the most part, those who might not be mobilized into more traditional forms of political activity. In this respect, protest supports the Audit values of inclusiveness and participation. That said, two aspects of political protest warrant some concern.

First, exclusive reliance on protest at the expense of engaging with government can have a corrosive effect on democracy. If activists prefer to remain outside the realm of the state, offering only critical perspectives and steadfastly refusing genuine offers to participate in constructive governmental processes, the eventual result is cynicism and distrust. Of course, this assumes that government makes genuine offers to engage with protest-oriented groups and to address their issues – an assumption that may not always hold. There are some groups whose perspectives are so critical of the status quo that they will not or cannot engage meaningfully with government. This becomes a concern only when protest replaces engagement as the dominant form of expression for most oppositional groups, which is certainly not the case in Canada today. Groups usually employ protest in concert with other tactics. Only a relatively small proportion of groups prefer protest to the exclusion of engagement.

A second concern arises when protest encompasses illegal activities. This question has been highlighted in recent years as antiglobalization protests have turned violent in Seattle, Quebec City, and elsewhere. In these instances, a relatively small number of protesters intent on showing their rage against the capitalist system have frustrated attempts by other activists to ensure that protests remain peaceful. It is important to distinguish between these violent illegal activities and peaceful acts of civil disobedience. Deliberately and non-violently breaking the law in order to protest an injustice is a well-established tradition within North American protest movements. For example, citizens opposed to insecticide fogging have blocked city streets in Winnipeg to prevent their neighbourhood from being sprayed. Such acts, although potentially illegal, are not violent and fall within the realm of civil disobedience.

The difficulty lies in determining where to draw the line between acceptable and unacceptable acts of illegal political protest. While most people today would accept that black civil rights activists in the United States were justified in defying segregation laws in the 1950s and 1960s, there is considerable disagreement as to whether it is acceptable for anti-abortion protesters to defy court orders and protest in front of abortion clinics, or for antilogging activists to blockade roads in order to prevent logging trucks from passing through. Most people would consider the civil rights activists' actions acceptable for two reasons: first, at least in retrospect, the laws against which the activists were protesting were undeniably unjust and discriminatory, and second, although the activists' acts were illegal, they were victimless. However, the merits of the issue being protested cannot safely be used as the criterion for judging the acceptability of civil disobedience, although they inevitably play into our judgments about such matters. Laws that are accepted by the majority – like the segregation laws – may well be judged unjust in retrospect. Protests against the laws were necessary to illustrate their unjust character. This leaves us with the criterion of whether the illegal act causes substantial harm to others, but judgments about the degree of harm caused to others are often subjective. Does the harm caused to women seeking abortions or loggers deprived of their livelihood for a day outweigh the protesters' entitlement to express their views?

In recent Canadian experience, protesters have made only limited use of civil disobedience tactics, and for the most part have restrained their actions to limit the impact on others to inconvenience. For example, traffic jams in the heart of the Toronto business district have been caused by antipoverty protesters, and highways have been blockaded by Aboriginal people. Even in the case of the violence at anti-globalization rallies, it is clear that the majority of protesters are trying to minimize the likelihood of violence occurring through techniques such as protest marshals. There are also isolated incidents of political violence like the burning of boats in northern New Brunswick in protest of the extension of crab fishing rights in the spring of 2003. Although troubling, these do not appear to signal a rise in the use of violent protest tactics. For these reasons we have little concern about the negative implications of protest activities.

Of greater concern than protesters' use of civil disobedience is the response of Canadian governments to dissenting voices from protesters.

In recent years, a number of incidents suggest that Canadian govern-ments are overly willing to use their power to monitor potential pro-testers, to limit voices of dissent, and to use inappropriate force to stop political protesters. Media reports indicate that the Toronto police department's intelligence unit regularly monitors antipoverty activists because it considers some antipoverty organizations that have been involved in clashes with police as "organized crime" groups (Lyons and Livesey 2001). In the days prior to the G8 summit held in Kananaskis, Alberta, in 2002, numerous media reports claimed that foreign activists were denied entry across Canadian borders so that they could not participate in protests at the summit. During the Summit of the Americas in Quebec city in April 2001, a 4.5-kilometre-long, three-metre-high fence was built to surround the entire summit area, effec-tively insuring that delegates to the summit would be insulated from the sight of protesters. Such occurrences suggest that Canadian gov-ernments have little respect for protesters' entitlement to express dis-senting views.

The clearest example of inappropriate policing of protests occurred in 1997, when RCMP officers used pepper spray on protesters at the Asia-Pacific Economic Cooperation (APEC) summit on the campus of the University of British Columbia. After holding hearings, the Com-mission for Public Complaints Against the RCMP issued a report list-ing a series of inappropriate police actions, including inappropriate arrest of protest organizers, ordering removal of protesters' signs and a Tibetan flag from student buildings, inappropriate use of pepper spray against demonstrators, and unjustifiable strip searches of women arrested at the protest (Commission for Public Complaints 2002). In short, the RCMP "imposed unreasonable restrictions on the freedom of movement, association and expression of law-abiding Canadian citizens" (Pue 2000, 6). Of particular concern in this instance was the political intent of the limitations – to protect world leaders from the sight of protesters, not to protect bystanders from vio-lence initiated by protesters. Since the APEC inquiry, Canadian police forces have apparently improved their planning for policing major protests, leading to fewer inappropriate uses of police force. Notably, in protests surrounding the 2002 G8 summit, Calgary police were con-gratulated for their use of "soft force," using regular uniformed police officers and officers on bicycles to monitor protests, with no police wearing riot gear in evidence. There were no major clashes between police and protesters on that occasion.

Nonetheless, the body of evidence regarding governments' decisions to use police forces (and occasionally the military and customs inspectors) to curtail protesters' freedom of expression is a matter of considerable concern. Democracy requires freedom of speech and assembly, and any moves to unnecessarily limit these fragile rights have the potential to weaken the quality of Canadian democracy substantially. Citizens must be on guard against such intrusions and inappropriate uses of state power.

Evaluating Advocacy Group Involvement in Elections, Litigation, and Protests

Critics of advocacy groups have tended to focus on the potential negative consequences of nontraditional advocacy techniques such as election advertising, litigation, and protest. Like these critics, we would be dismayed if these activities were the mainstay of Canadian advocacy groups. But the evidence we have presented in Chapter 6 and this chapter suggest that engaging with the institutions of representative government remains the central focus of advocacy in this country. We believe democracy benefits from having other routes available to advocates when they believe engaging directly with government has been or will be fruitless.

Without alternative channels, advocacy groups are unable to find ways to broaden the parameters of public debates, to check governments' decisions against guarantees of fundamental rights and freedoms, and to articulate discontent. Taken as a whole, these nontraditional advocacy techniques widen the scope of participation in Canadian democracy, and by bringing different voices into the conversation, expand the scope of democratic discussion in this country.

We view efforts to curtail groups' use of election advertising, litigation, and protest with considerable suspicion. In most instances, we believe that this broadening of the scope of democratic discussion is of essential importance. Only when a compelling case can be made that public safety or the integrity of representative institutions is at risk should limits be placed on these activities.

Chapter 7

Strengths

- Advocacy group participation in elections appears to broaden the scope of issues discussed during election campaigns and presents little threat to political parties.
- Through rulings governing standing and intervener status in court cases, the Canadian courts have facilitated advocacy group litigation.
- The Court Challenges Program has also facilitated advocacy group litigation.
- The Charter protects protesters' rights of freedom of speech and assembly.
- For the most part, protesters in Canada avoid illegal and violent tactics.

Weaknesses

- Citizens should be able to access information about who is contributing to advocacy groups that advertise during elections, and that information should be available before election day.
- Governments have demonstrated an alarming tendency to criminalize and restrict legitimate political dissent.

WHO PREVAILS?

8

In previous chapters, we found that some groups face greater obstacles to mobilization than do others, and that groups with fewer resources sometimes find it more difficult to gain access to decision makers. In this chapter, we pursue this line of inquiry to its logical conclusion. Which interests tend to prevail in policy decisions? Are Canadian governments consistently more responsive to some interests over others? What factors affect governments' responsiveness to groups?

The Audit value at stake in this discussion is that of responsiveness, as well as the related issue of equity. Ideally, in a democratic system, we want government to be responsive to the opinions and interests of citizens. But when citizens are not unanimous in their opinions, or when competing interests come into play, government must make choices about which groups win and which groups lose. This is a necessary function of government, and one that does not necessarily detract from the government's responsiveness to societal interests. Where these choices become problematic, however, is when government consistently favours one set of interests over all others. In such a situation, government is responsive only to a limited segment of society, and is consequently inequitable in its distribution of resources.

The question of "who prevails" lies at the very heart of the study of politics. The pluralist view holds that interests compete, and that no segment of society consistently wins or loses these competitions, but this contention is highly controversial. Critics arguing from a variety of other perspectives contend that liberal democracies perpetuate relationships of inequality, so that government decisions consistently reflect the preferences of more powerful segments of society. In this view, men's interests generally win out over women's, majority ethnic groups win out over minorities, or in the Canadian case anglophone interests win out over francophone. The most frequent critique, however, holds that business interests – or the interests of the wealthy – win out over all other interests. For instance, in his major study of business group organization in Canada, Coleman (1988, 4) states that "all groups and categories of citizen are not equal ... There is a systematic bias in the Canadian system, which consistently gives the business community a better hearing and considers its demands and proposals more seriously when policies are being designed."

The argument that business interests win out over all others is a powerful critique of the egalitarian promise of liberal democracy. To the extent that business prevails, it is not simply a consequence of a government's ideological preference for business, although that may well factor into the equation. Rather, powerful underlying reasons incline governments of all political stripes to adapt public policy in the interests of business. First, businesses and wealthy individuals have money and social status, which together increase the perceived legitimacy of the group. This allows business groups to pursue insider strategies such as lobbying, as was discussed in Chapter 6. Second, and even more significant, liberal democracies rely to a great extent on business to produce wealth. What is in the interests of Canadian business, then, is to a considerable extent in the interests of the Canadian government, which relies on business to fuel the economy, to create the prosperity that keeps Canadian voters content, and to generate the incomes that governments tax in order to fulfill their mandates. Consequently business has an undeniable advantage over other interests in gaining the ear of government. As Coleman (1988, 4) notes, "Nothing could be more natural in a capitalist liberal democracy."

Due to the unique place of business interests in liberal democracies, we have chosen to focus our analysis of "who prevails" on business interests. Are business interests consistently successful in gaining the ear of Canadian governments, or are other interests also able to prevail under some circumstances? We go on to consider the factors that determine which interests will prevail.

In this discussion, we rely heavily on studies that use a "policy community" approach to understanding how organized interests affect public policy (see Coleman and Skogstad 1990). This literature defines a policy community to include "all actors or potential actors with a direct or indirect interest in a policy area or function who share a common 'policy focus' and who, with varying degrees of influence, shape policy outcomes over the long run" (25). Within the policy community, we find the *subgovernment,* which is composed of government agencies, interest associations, and other social organizations that make public policy, and the *attentive public,* which is made up of interest associations that are not regularly included in policy making, relevant media, and interested and expert individuals. Unlike the subgovernment, which develops policy, the attentive public follows and attempts to influence public policy, but does not participate regularly in its development. The distinction between the subgovernment and the attentive public is useful because it demonstrates that "in any policy community, there are two levels of exclusion. Social or state actors may belong to the community, but not be included in the sub-government; or they may be subject to a policy but not included as part of the attentive public" (Coleman 1994, 276).

The policy community approach is particularly helpful because it rejects the notion that governments *always* act in the interest of one group, the notion that governments are *always* neutral arbitrators between competing interests. Rather, the policy community approach directs our attention away from these macro-level conceptions of the state as a unified actor, suggesting instead that we focus our inquiry at the level of individual government agencies or departments. According to the policy community approach, these meso-level government actors will have different and sometimes competing interests and will vary in their capacity to impose their policy preferences. In our view, this literature offers a more nuanced and empirically supported conception of the state than do approaches that treat the state as a unified whole with consistent preferences and capacities. The policy community conception will inform our discussion of which interests prevail in the development of public policy.

Does Business Always Win?

In the early 1970s, political scientist Robert Presthus (1973) undertook a major study of the representation of interests in the Canadian political process. He concluded that interest group leaders comprised part of a Canadian elite that dominated decision making. This pattern of elite accommodation, he argued, was instrumental in maintaining national unity but also formed a closed system of decision making. When he included interest group leaders as members of a national elite, Presthus was referring mainly to business and professional leaders, but secondarily to leaders of welfare and other groups. Since Presthus published this landmark study, the number of groups active on the Canadian political scene has proliferated, and much of that proliferation has involved the emergence of citizens' groups. More recent accounts suggest that the closed system of elite accommodation began to decline gradually just as Presthus published his study. Elite accommodation was challenged by the proliferation of nonbusiness interest groups, the rise of television (which allowed groups to mobilize support for their causes), and the centralization of government decision making, which imposed more rational criteria on decision making than had been the case in the past (Pross, cited in Thorburn 1985, 11).

If we accept that the Canadian advocacy group system has become more complex and more diverse, we are left with the question of whether business still prevails. Business benefits from an exchange in personnel between business and government, as former politicians and senior civil servants take up corporate directorships and senior business figures enter electoral politics (Brooks and Stritch 1991, 209-10). And business interests certainly have more financial resources available to them than do most citizens' groups. The most recent comprehensive study of business associations' total spending patterns was done over twenty years ago. In the 1980 study, business associations spent $575,000 on average, with the largest associations spending in excess of $5 million annually (Coleman 1988, 41). There is no reason to believe that these figures have declined over the past twenty years. Only the very largest citizens' groups report revenues anywhere near this magnitude. In 2000 the Council of Canadians raised about $2 million from its members and supporters, and the Canadian Taxpayers Federation, which raises funds from individuals and small businesses, raised $3.2 million in 2001. Notably, however, these groups need to reinvest significant portions of the monies they raise back into fundraising campaigns. Of its $3.2 million budget, the CTF earmarked half for fundraising (Falconer 2001, 43, 55). Having more money can allow groups to maintain a prominent presence in political circles by hiring lobbyists, sponsoring events that gain media attention, and placing advertisements in support of their cause.

In surveys, business leaders and leaders of civil society groups respond similarly when asked whether they influence government. Generally, both groups feel that they have little influence. Just over one-third of business leaders believe that government decision makers are willing to consider industry representations in their decisions (PPF 2001, 5), while a slightly larger proportion (37 percent) of executives of civil society organizations perceived that their groups were successful in putting the interests of their constituents on the policy agenda (Embuldeniya 2001, vii). In the same way, only 30 percent of leaders of human rights organizations perceived their groups to be effective (Howe and Johnson 1995, 254). In this view, business is on an equal footing with other groups in its dealings with government.

On the other hand, governmental decision makers believe that they are relatively more open to business interests. In surveys undertaken in both the early 1980s and 2000 that compared the perceptions of business and government representatives, the government representatives perceived themselves to be much more open to business influence than did the business interests themselves (see Stanbury 1986, 175; PPF 2001, 5). Similarly, a survey of city councillors in Winnipeg in the early 1980s found that they perceived business to be by far the most influential lobby, followed distantly by neighbourhood associations and unions (Chekki and Toews 1985, 12-13).

Despite executives' protests that they have little influence over public policy, some evidence points in the opposite direction. The president and CEO of one of the largest business lobby groups – the Council of Chief Executives (formerly the Business Council on National Issues, or BCNI) – claims that business has had greater influence over public policy since the early 1980s than it has over the past century: "Look at what we stand for and look at what all the governments, all the major parties including Reform have done and what they want to do. They have adopted the agendas we've been fighting for in the past two decades" (Thomas D'Aquino, cited in Newman 1998, 159). Supporting his claim that "Canada's business establishment deliberately began setting Ottawa's political agenda," Newman cites the example of revisions to the Combines Act, which regulates the formation of monopolies. The BCNI spent $1 million to hire its own team of twenty-five lawyers to draft new legislation, which was then adopted as the new competition law in 1995. This, says Newman, "was the only time in the history of capitalism that any country allowed its anti-monopoly legislation to be written by the very people it was meant to police" (155). Beyond this specific example, one could argue that low rates of corporate taxation, macroeconomic policies focused on deficit and debt reduction, and the existence of significant government subsidies for some industrial sectors point to the substantial influence business exerts over all levels of government in Canada.

Even though business possesses a considerable advantage over other interests in the policy process, its influence is by no means absolute. First, many different, and often diverging, interests are encompassed within the Canadian business community. Industries that have benefited from tariffs do not share the enthusiasm of export-oriented industries for free trade; railways believe that long-distance truckers receive unfair subsidies in the form of well-maintained highways; companies compete with one another for government subsidies and favourable regulations. As a result of the many conflicting interests among industries and businesses, a significant portion of the business community's lobbying activity is focused on competition between business interests rather than competition between business and other interests.

Second, even though over the past two decades the business community has exercised considerable influence over the federal and many provincial governments' macroeconomic policies, there have been significant instances in which business interests have *not* prevailed. This conforms to the expectations of the policy community approach, which predicts that government will be more independent of business interests in some sectors than in others. The regulation of tobacco products is an excellent illustration of the ebb and flow of business influence over government. In an article chronicling the efforts of the tobacco lobby (mainly cigarette manufacturers) and anti-smoking organizations' efforts to influence public policy, Pross and Stewart (1994) note that until the 1970s, the tobacco lobby faced little organized opposition. This changed with the formation of the Non-Smokers' Rights Association, which lobbied government for more stringent regulation of tobacco products, limits on where cigarettes could be smoked, and programs to discourage smoking. By the mid-1980s, the antismoking lobby had changed public opinion so completely that tobacco regulation came to be seen as a health issue rather than an industry-based economic issue. As a consequence, anti-smoking groups were able to convince the federal government to pass legislation forbidding tobacco companies from sponsoring sporting or cultural events, banning advertising of tobacco products, and requiring health warnings on cigarette packages.

Pross and Stewart (1994) attribute this to the antismoking lobby's ability to build coalitions of antismoking and health-oriented groups and the increasing sophistication of these groups in influencing both public opinion and legislators. These groups also found strong allies within government, particularly in the Ministry of Health, which had an obvious interest in reducing smoking. This represents an instance of a subgovernment that perceives its interests to be in opposition of those of business, and develops public policy accordingly. Even so, Pross and Stewart argue that the tobacco lobby was able to gain access to officials, thereby slowing implementation of some of these measures and convincing the federal government to lower its tax on cigarettes. Despite these successes, the antismoking lobby prevailed over a very wealthy and well-organized business lobby.

There are other notable examples of citizens' groups successfully challenging business interests in recent years. Environmental groups in British Columbia lobbied government, engaged in extended protests, and organized an international boycott in order to push the provincial government into significant changes in forestry practices and greater protection for old-growth forests (Cashore et al. 2001; Stanbury 2000). An international coalition of nongovernmental organizations, with the Council of Canadians playing a key role, was able to exert enough pressure on national governments to prevent ratification of the Multilateral Agreement on Investment, a major international agreement that would have protected the interests of international capital (Kobrin 1998; Warby 1999). The federal government ratified the Kyoto Accord in 2002 over the objections of the oil and gas industry. A study of business groups' campaigns to prevent ratification concluded that the business lobby's inability to win public opinion to its side despite an extensive advertising and lobbying campaign was a crucial element of this defeat (Macdonald 2003).

In each of these situations, the nonbusiness groups had fewer resources at their disposal than did the corporate interests they challenged, yet they were able to achieve their policy objectives. The common element in all of these cases is the ability of the groups involved to mobilize public opinion on their side. To the extent that groups are able to garner public support, they have a powerful tool at their disposal for convincing governments of the merits of their case. In this respect, citizens' groups under some circumstances enjoy an advantage over corporate interests. Moreover, in many of the above instances citizens' groups found allies in government. Government agencies with interests in fostering public health or environmental protection became allies for citizens' groups and helped them achieve their policy objectives, even in the face of opposition from business interests. Thus, although business enjoys a number of advantages in its dealings with government, it does not *always* prevail.

What Determines Interest Group Effectiveness?

This brings us to the question of what factors make interest groups effective. The most obvious definition of effectiveness in this context is achieving a group's desired policy outcome. Nevertheless, for many groups, successfully mobilizing and making their members' voices heard in the policy process is considered an achievement. For example, a study of antipoverty activists in Montreal in the 1970s argues that the process of mobilization into a movement was itself a great success for the activists involved. For them, the movement "was a place where those who faced oppression from the wider society could redefine themselves and could become actors rather than victims" (Kruzynski and Shragge 1999, 337). In fact, for many social movement activists, mobilization, maintenance of a nonhierarchical democratic internal culture, representation of the diversity of the movement, and firm adherence to the movement's core principles are more important than external successes.

For most advocacy groups, however, effectiveness is understood to mean having some impact on public policy decisions. Success in achieving policy change is contingent on a variety of factors, many of which are beyond a group's own control. For example, international events such as wars or global economic crises may heighten government awareness of certain subjects and provide some groups with windows of opportunity for change on their policy issue. Conversely, these events may shift attention away from other issues, making it more difficult for other groups to attract government attention and support. Similarly, international agreements on trade or human rights may inhibit or facilitate a group's ability to affect policy change by limiting what actions governments may actually take on particular issues.

That said, most factors that determine the degree of a group's success or failure can be traced back to the nature of the Canadian state and the individuals who govern it or to the individual groups themselves. State factors include the ideological orientations of the governing party and the administrative capacity of critical government agencies. Even the presence of sympathetic individuals in key decision-making positions may affect a group's degree of influence. Characteristics of the group itself that contribute to its ability to exert influence include its access to skills, information, and expertise sought by the state, the size and degree of representativeness of its membership base, and the degree to which its positions are supported by general public opinion. Each of these factors will be discussed in turn.

Party in Government/Orientation of Government

The ideological orientation of the party in government can potentially make a tremendous difference to the ability of groups to affect policy outcomes. Even though governments are not monolithic actors and various departments pursue their own interests and agendas, eventually the party in government must mediate between competing interests. Anecdotal evidence suggests that different political parties tend to favour different interests when in government. In the Canadian experience, this has been illustrated most clearly in changes to or from a New Democratic Party government. The NDP is a left-leaning party that has connections with trade unions, women's organizations, environmental groups, and a variety of social justice organizations. NDP governments stand out as exceptions to the general domination of Canadian politics by centre and centre-right parties at the national and provincial level.

The election of NDP governments in British Columbia, Saskatchewan, Manitoba, and Ontario created opportunities for a number of rights-oriented and left-leaning citizens' groups. For instance, Boyce et al. (2001, ch. 6) outline the experience of disability groups trying to influence legislation concerning the legal status of individuals with mental health disabilities. When the NDP came to government in Ontario in 1990, groups representing these individuals were allowed considerable influence over policy and even played a role in drafting legislation. After the Conservatives defeated the NDP in 1995, the legislation was reworked significantly to reverse many of the disability organizations' policy gains. Similarly, Cashore et al. (2001) argue that the election of an NDP government in BC was key to opening the door for environmental groups to influence forestry policy. In his study of the Ontario Women's Directorate, Malloy (1999) notes that the feminist movement was consulted more extensively during the period when the NDP was in government than it had been in the past or has been subsequently. Studies of child care policy have reached the same conclusion, with the election of NDP governments in BC and Ontario leading to changes favouring nonprofit child care providers (Collier 2001). Studies of child care advocacy groups in Alberta, with its perpetual Conservative government, conclude that advocates of nonprofit child care have tended not to be able to influence public policy, while owners of for-profit child care centres have enjoyed reasonable access to government. This is attributed at least in part to the ideological orientation of the provincial government (Fletcher 1994; Langford 2001).

These examples show that election of an NDP government tends to improve the potential for left-leaning citizens' groups to influence public policy. As a corollary, election of Conservative and, in some cases, Liberal governments improves the potential for business and other right-leaning groups to exercise influence. That said, these are not absolute certainties. For instance, welfare rights groups complained that their ability to influence policy was less under the Ontario NDP than it had been under the preceding Liberal government (Sheldrick 1998), and many unions became extremely disenchanted with the Ontario NDP as it embarked on a program of deficit reduction.

The orientation of the government also has an effect on groups' ability to influence public policy. During the 1970s and early 1980s, the federal Liberal government was oriented toward promoting social equality and as part of this was clearly open to influence by citizens' interest groups, in many cases providing funding to the very groups attempting to influence it. Since 1993 the same party has been in power but has been focused primarily on eliminating the budget deficit and providing sound fiscal management. As a result, groups perceive the government to be much less open to influence than it was in the past. Not only has the federal government significantly reduced funding for many groups, but it has also reduced the kind of access groups enjoy. For instance, during the Trudeau era, the National Action Committee on the Status of Women could usually expect good attendance from cabinet ministers and government MPs at its annual lobby day on Parliament Hill. This is no longer the case, and the same is true for many of the other "compensatory" groups we have discussed in this study.

CAPACITY OF GOVERNMENT AGENCIES

Although the orientation of the government as a whole affects the ability of groups to influence outcomes, the policy community approach reminds us that most interactions between groups and governments take place within a particular policy sector. This means that the groups deal primarily with one or two government departments. Within any government, there can be tremendous variation among departments, in terms of both their policy objectives and how well equipped the departments are to pursue those objectives. Some departments may have a clear sense of mandate, and will try to use interest groups as a means of pursuing their objectives. For instance, they might fund groups whose views they favour and ensure that members of such groups are well represented in policy discussions. An example of this is the federal government's role in sponsoring antipoverty organizations in the 1970s (Haddow 1990) or multicultural groups that support federal multiculturalism policy (Pal 1993; Kobayashi 2000). In other instances, government departments have a less clear sense of mandate on an issue, and may lack much of the information necessary to develop public policy in the area. Such departments are more open to influence from interest groups that provide relevant data and exert pressure. For example, the Ministry of Finance has tended to rely heavily on financial institutions to provide information needed to develop federal regulations in that industry. It follows from this that a group's ability to influence public policy is partially dependent on the orientation and capacity of relevant government departments, as well as on the group's placement within the relevant policy community.

ACCESS TO GOVERNMENT DECISION MAKERS

In the example of tobacco regulation outlined above, one of the most important reasons the tobacco lobby was able to slow the implementation of regulations and convince the federal government to drop its tobacco tax was the group's access to key decision makers. Not coincidentally, during this period the chief lobbyist for the tobacco industry was William Neville, who was also a friend of and speechwriter for Brian Mulroney, then the prime minister. While such high-level political connections can potentially be very important to gaining access to key decision makers, other sorts of connections may also be helpful. For instance, representatives of disability groups emphasize the importance of inside contacts, noting "we have a couple of people who have worked in different ministries who have disabilities themselves and who are interested in being our inside people. They can get us into a lot of places that we couldn't get otherwise" (in Boyce et al. 2001, 61). Similarly, the gay and lesbian rights group EGALE attributes much of its success to supporters in major government positions.

SKILLS, INFORMATION, AND EXPERTISE

Groups require an understanding of the policy process in order to know whom to contact and what strategy to pursue. One way a group can convince government to pursue the policies it suggests is by providing information government needs. In many instances, industry associations have ready – and sometimes exclusive – access to statistics and other data needed by public servants to develop policy (Pross

1992, 196). Moreover, government decision makers may defer to groups possessing expertise related to the subject manner at hand. An example is the federal government's treatment of the medical establishment in the matter of regulating assisted reproductive technologies. In his study of this policy process, Montpetit (2003b) concludes that one of the factors that permitted groups representing physicians to prevail in this policy arena was politicians' tendency to defer to medical expertise and to the capacity of respected professions, like doctors, to self-regulate.

Size and Representativeness of the Group

When groups are trying to convince policy makers to accept their perspective on an issue, they can often do so more effectively when they can claim to represent a large number of Canadian voters, to be highly representative of a group that will be affected by the policy, or to speak for a range of affected interests. Chapter 4 documented the tremendous variation among Canadian advocacy groups with respect to their size and representativeness. Those with larger and more involved memberships or with some capacity to consult widely within their constituency have a greater representational claim to make when engaging with government. One technique groups use to enhance their claim of representativeness is to form coalitions of groups that share the same view on a policy issue. Not only do the groups benefit from shared resources, but coalitions can also help to convince decision makers of a broad base of support for a policy direction. For example, advocates of firearms regulation formed coalitions with groups representing victims of violence and the Canadian Association of Chiefs of Police in order to strengthen their claims (Rathjen and Montpetit 1999), and antismoking advocates strengthened their hand significantly by drawing the Canadian Cancer Society into their advocacy campaign (Pross and Stewart 1994).

Public Opinion

Finally, the ability of a group to mobilize public opinion is often crucial to its success. As we noted above, this was the case with environmentalists' influence over BC forest policy, antismoking groups' success in convincing the federal government to regulate tobacco products, and the defeat of the Multilateral Agreement on Investment (MAI) by a loose international coalition of nongovernmental organizations. All of these examples point to the growing importance of indirect lobbying for various organizations. To influence government, they must first mobilize public opinion. The emergence of the Internet has created an additional channel for reaching the public. Unlike traditional mass media, the Internet allows groups to communicate with the interested public in an unmediated way, so a message is delivered in its entirety and in the form the group chooses. The Internet was credited with a significant role in defeating the MAI. While recognizing the potential importance of the Internet, it must be noted that users have to actively search out a group's materials on the Web, whereas coverage on television or in newspapers brings the group's perspective to the wider public.

Evaluating Who Prevails

This brings us to the final question of how responsive Canadian governments are to groups, which has no simple answer. As we indicated above, there is variation not only among governments but also within governments. For the most part, Canadian governments are neither entirely responsive nor entirely unresponsive to groups.

From an Audit perspective, this last statement is encouraging. Given that groups play an important role in transmitting citizens' views to government, it would be undesirable if Canadian governments were entirely closed to interest group input. But at the same time, it would be equally objectionable to conclude that Canadian governments are not independent of influential interest groups. Governments possess democratic mandates (flawed though they may be), and are the only institutions charged with the responsibility of balancing competing societal interests. If governments cede this responsibility and listen only to narrowly based interests, then democracy is not well served.

However, little evidence supports this notion. In fact, comparative public policy studies have suggested that Canadian governments are relatively independent of interest groups, particularly when compared to the government of the United States. In the American case, "Political structures are so accessible to interest groups [that] laws adopted by Congress and signed by the President are sometimes a conglomeration of concessions to various special interests" (Rosenau 1994, 300). In Canada, in contrast, government institutions are less permeable to organized interests and have the capacity to maintain independence and broker logical and reasoned compromises between competing interests. This does not necessarily imply that all government policies are logical and reasoned, but the structure of Canadian institutions holds out that possibility, all other things being equal. The strength of the executive in Canadian legislatures provides a means through which governments are insulated from excessive interest group influence.

Our overview of the capacity of various advocacy groups in this chapter leads us to a tentative conclusion that the responsiveness of Canadian governments to groups is adequate. Business groups occupy a privileged position and frequently experience greater responsiveness, but this situation is virtually unavoidable in a capitalist society. Other groups can influence the policy process, and the overall trend is in the direction of increasing responsiveness. In general terms, there appears to be a reasonable balance between over- and underresponsiveness on the part of Canadian governments.

That said, we must recall our conclusions in the previous chapters that groups with more resources are more likely to mobilize, and that resources also affect the tactics employed by groups and their potential effectiveness. It follows from this that there will be inequities in patterns of government responsiveness. Criticisms that the wealthy win out over the poor, that men win out over women, that adults win out over children, and that the able-bodied win out over the disabled reflect the imbalances in resources that, in turn, make governments more responsive to higher status and privileged groups. The source of this problem lies more in barriers to mobilization and access than in systematic patterns of favouritism among Canadian governments.

Chapter 8

Strengths

- Canadian governments generally have achieved a reasonable balance between over- and underresponsiveness to organized interests.
- Although business remains privileged in its relationship with the state, it has been challenged to some extent by other actors that have emerged since the early 1970s.

Weaknesses

- Business continues to enjoy greater state responsiveness than other interests, thereby creating inequities.
- Inequities in resources and in access to decision makers carry through to inequities in patterns of government responsiveness.

9 ENHANCING THE DEMOCRATIC ROLE OF ADVOCACY GROUPS

As we have seen, the general category of advocacy groups encompasses a remarkably diverse set of political actors. From small collectives of concerned parents lobbying for changes to education policy to large, mass-membership organizations calling for changes to trade policy, and from antipoverty groups to business lobby organizations, groups play a prominent role in most areas of government decision making at every level of jurisdiction. Previous chapters have tried to give readers a sense of the great diversity of these groups in terms of their internal organization, objectives, methods of operation, and policy impact. As we strive to draw conclusions about the role groups play in contemporary Canadian democracy, we are well aware of the difficulties inherent in making blanket judgments about such a varied collection of organizations. Our task is made all the more challenging by the relative absence of comprehensive studies of advocacy groups in this country, which forces our analysis to rely instead on anecdotal evidence and existing case studies. This speaks to the need for more research on this subject.

This chapter revisits the benchmarks set out in Chapter 1, focusing on the extent to which groups enhance the core Audit values of participation, responsiveness, and inclusiveness, as well as addressing the extent to which groups contribute to the general quality of contemporary Canadian democracy. Following from this, we engage in the prescriptive aspect of the audit, making recommendations about the best practices that groups can follow in their internal organization and efforts to influence public policy, and about the actions governments can take to engage constructively with groups and to create an environment that fosters desirable qualities in group activity.

Participation

As we noted in Chapter 2, one of the potential benefits groups offer to democracy is their ability to mobilize citizens to participate in the political system. Three aspects of participation are of particular salience for groups: extent of participation mobilized, equality among different societal groups, and quality of participation.

From our analysis in Chapter 3, we concluded that in comparison to other countries, a large number of Canadian citizens are highly active in advocacy groups. Eleven percent of Canadians claim to have been involved in an "interest group" and almost 40 percent claim membership in organizations that may at times assume an advocacy role. Furthermore, the number of people involved in such groups has increased over the past few decades. This increase is reflected in the explosion of both the number and variety of advocacy groups active at all three levels of government in Canada.

Despite this proliferation of group activity it is important to recognize the challenges that limit the mobilization of some interests. We examined this issue in Chapter 5, and concluded that groups with access to fewer resources – monetary and other – were at a distinct disadvantage when it came to mobilization. The poor, children, and new Canadians, among others, face greater challenges than the wealthy or the socially established. In addition, diffuse interests, such as consumers, are much more difficult to mobilize than more focused and immediate interests, particularly when selective benefits are at stake.

We also confirmed that advocacy group activists are drawn from similar backgrounds to members of political parties, the more standard vehicles for political engagement. Generally, both types of organization tend to be dominated by older, white, well-educated individuals. This observation questions the claim that advocacy groups are highly inclusive. However, it should be noted that this is not true for all types of groups: women's groups and environmental organizations are much more socially inclusive than others, most likely because they are structured around principles that emphasize equality of access and participation. This suggests that compensatory organizations play an important role in offsetting the democratic deficits found in other institutions in our political system.

Chapter 4 highlighted some of the challenges faced by advocacy groups themselves in their efforts to be participatory organizations. This goal is often affected by the philosophy of the group and the financial resources available to it. Staff-led organizations place little value on member participation and consequently make little effort to establish participatory internal structures. For those groups rooted in equality-seeking social movements, participation is a more salient issue. Unfortunately, providing opportunities for participation in a group's decision-making process is expensive, especially given Canada's size and diverse linguistic, social, and economic makeup. Despite the best intentions, not all groups are able to overcome these participatory challenges without government assistance, a point that we return to in our recommendations below.

Although rates of participation in advocacy groups are relatively high, we are concerned about "chequebook" participation and the growing trend toward the creation of nonmembership groups such as the Canadian Taxpayers Federation or Greenpeace Canada. From the perspective of democracy, this trend is problematic in two respects. First, active participation in an advocacy group has the potential to enhance democratic citizenship, as it engages individuals in political discussion and activity. If participation is limited to financial support, there is no opportunity for engaging in the political discussion or the give-and-take of collective decision making that we see as salutary activities. Second, groups with donors rather than members have little accountability to their constituency. Their claim to speak on behalf of a group is weaker than claims made by participatory groups. As such, these groups have less to offer the public discussion of an issue. This leads to the criterion of responsiveness.

Responsiveness

When applied to groups, the Audit value of responsiveness refers to two quite different things. The first dimension of responsiveness relates to how responsive groups themselves are, both to their members and to the broader constituency they purport to represent. This dimension was the focus of Chapter 4, which found that Canadian groups vary widely in their degree of responsiveness to their members, supporters, and constituencies. Unfortunately, few groups have established mechanisms that enable members to engage actively in setting policy, to raise questions about the strategies or tactics employed by the organization, or to hold its executive to account through democratic elections. Instead, decision making is frequently left to the group leaders, sometimes guided by periodic surveys of the members. Accountability, particularly in large staff-led organizations, is limited to a group member's decision to leave the organization and no longer contribute financially to the group. Those groups that do maintain structures for accountability are often responding to the internal democratic pressures found in compensatory organizations or to external pressures from government decision makers to prove their responsiveness to their constituency.

The second dimension of responsiveness has to do with governments' willingness to listen to the perspectives that groups bring to bear on public policy, and to give these perspectives fair consideration in determining public policy. This is one of the most difficult aspects of group involvement to measure, and only tentative conclusions can be drawn. In the discussion of types of group activities and governments' responses in Chapters 6 and 7, we observed that groups' access to governments has not changed significantly over the past decade, although we did note a potentially worrisome trend toward government consultation with individuals rather than groups. Having considered the effectiveness of groups in influencing public policy in Chapter 8, we concluded that Canadian governments have been reasonably successful in reaching a balance between under- and overresponsiveness to organized interests. Although most groups would – and do – express dissatisfaction with their ability to influence government, the interests of democracy remain well-served when governments mediate among competing interests. Of greater concern is the tendency for some interests, particularly business, to gain greater access and consequently greater responsiveness than do others. This phenomenon is discussed below under the heading of inclusiveness.

We did, however, identify several weaknesses related to governments' responsiveness toward groups. The widespread use of paid lobbyists allows wealthier groups more extensive access to government decision makers, creating inequities in the patterns of responsiveness. In a similar vein, we found evidence that groups sometimes lack the capacity and resources to participate effectively in consultation processes. As government funding to groups has declined, this phenomenon has become more pervasive and a greater source of concern. In addition, some government consultation processes are designed not to solicit input but rather to legitimize decisions that have already been made. Finally, and perhaps most worrisome, Canadian governments have over the past decade demonstrated an alarming tendency to criminalize and restrict legitimate political dissent. This may limit not only basic civil liberties, which are crucial to democracy, but also the ability of government to hear from all segments of society, including those that choose protest as their way of communicating with government.

Inclusiveness

One of the prime concerns when examining the role of advocacy groups in contemporary Canadian democracy is the extent to which group representation to government is inclusive of the diversity of Canadian society. In one sense, concern for inclusiveness leads us to ask whether all relevant interests are mobilized and given a fair hearing, or whether some segments of society, notably wealthy business interests, consistently receive preferential treatment in response to their representations to government. In a second respect, inclusiveness relates to the extent to which those segments of society that have not received adequate representation within the electoral arena – such as women, visible minorities, gays and lesbians, and the disabled – are able to use interest group representation to compensate for their lack of influence within the traditional institutions of government.

With respect to the first concern, we concluded that business does enjoy a privileged place among interest groups. Groups like industry associations that represent selective concerns and enjoy extensive financial resources are better able to mobilize, to gain access to decision makers, and to make their case effectively. That said, business does not always prevail when its interests conflict with those of other groups. In particular, the public interest organizations that have proliferated since the 1970s have been effective in challenging the political dominance of business in several respects. Although this does not necessarily create a perfect balance, it does introduce some degree of equity into the political system.

Mobilization through interest groups and social movement organizations has substantially increased the representation of marginalized groups in the political system. Over the past thirty years, women, members of ethnic minorities, gays and lesbians, and the disabled, among others, have gone from being almost entirely absent from political decision making to being taken seriously as significant players, at least in some sectors. This would not have been possible without group mobilization. Employing a combination of protest, lobbying, and litigation tactics, these groups have transformed both the advocacy group system in Canada and the lives of many citizens. Shifts in the political climate and reductions in government funding for many of these organizations, however, have had the effect of making these groups' voices less prominent on the national political stage in recent years. To the extent that this is the case, the inclusiveness of Canadian democracy has been reduced.

Recommendations for Groups

Our audit has evaluated both the internal practices of groups and the various ways in which governments relate to groups. The first recommendations based on this study are intended to assist groups in furthering the development of democratic culture and values in their internal organizations and activities. We are well aware of the limitations of exhorting groups to employ various practices, but any audit of group participation in Canadian politics would be incomplete without recommendations directed toward the groups themselves. We then turn our attention to governments, and examine the actions they can take in providing financial support to groups, in fostering productive exchanges and relationships with groups while developing public policy, and in regulating groups.

Recommendations for Internal Group Organization

Advocacy groups represent important links between citizens and governments and, as such, they perform a crucial function in Canadian democracy. However, we maintain that their contribution is greatest when they adhere to democratic principles in their own organizational structures. Internally democratic organizations are structured in such a way that members can participate meaningfully in the running of the group and that the group's leadership can be held accountable to the membership through regular elections. Above all else, we encourage groups to recognize their important role within Canadian democracy. Groups should be aware that they have the capacity to contribute to the quality of Canadian democracy by providing participatory opportunities for their members.

As noted in Chapter 4, active participation in advocacy groups depends on both the openness of group membership and the range of participatory opportunities in which members can engage. From our perspective as auditors, we believe that each group needs to find a balance between the size of its membership as an indicator of its openness and the opportunities for participation in group governance and decision making. Meaningful involvement in the activities of a group produces important spinoffs for democratic values and other forms of political engagement, and we encourage groups to provide as many opportunities for participation as possible. Admittedly, the costs of maintaining democratic structures in large membership organizations can be prohibitive. Furthermore, the requirement for widespread participation in decision making limits a group's flexibility to respond quickly to new policy developments. As a result, many large organizations provide only limited opportunities for participation. While we recognize that not all groups seek to be internally democratic, we recommend that those that do look to the model provided by the Council of Canadians, whose structure presents members with opportunities to participate in local chapters while still allowing the national leadership considerable autonomy to set national policy priorities.

A second key requirement for internally democratic organizations is that the leadership of the group be responsive and accountable to its members, supporters, and constituencies. Accountability measures that we expect in democratically organized associations include the formal election of executives, the holding of annual meetings, and regular communication between the executive and members through newsletters, e-mail, or web pages. As we have noted, the rise in staff-led groups with chequebook members is of concern because of the difficulty of ensuring responsiveness in these organizations. But there are many ways for these groups to consult with their members and provide them with opportunities to participate in those debates that may pertain to them. We encourage such groups to survey their members on a regular basis and update them through mailings or newsletters. If nothing else, members will then have opportunities to learn more about the activities of those groups that they support.

While not all groups have the resources to engage in these communication exercises, new technologies such as the Internet represent important opportunities for groups to enhance their degree of responsiveness. These technological developments have reduced some of the costs associated with communication, as the Internet can be used to promote group activities and provide information as well as to communicate with members. We recommend that advocacy groups take advantage of these technologies, creating websites to advertise their activities and policy positions and using e-mail as a quick and inexpensive way to consult and maintain contact with their membership.

Finally, inclusiveness is one of the most basic principles of democracy and we would argue that the internal democracy of advocacy groups is enhanced when they are composed of the broad range of individuals that they claim to represent. Admittedly the membership base of some groups is more diverse than that of others; groups that play a role in addressing the democratic deficits in other Canadian institutions face greater demands to be inclusive than those that have no such mandate. Nonetheless, we would recommend that national Canadian advocacy organizations make serious efforts to represent region, language, ethnicity, and gender in their internal structures. Regional and local groups should also pay attention to these qualities depending upon their own particular contexts.

RECOMMENDATIONS FOR ADVOCACY GROUP TACTICS

This audit has paid considerable attention to the strategies used by advocacy groups to attract the attention of government and the general public. As outlined in Chapters 6 and 7, groups employ different tactics depending upon their ideological predispositions, their goals, and their resources. In general, we support groups' efforts to engage with government by lobbying, participating in consultative exercises, advertising in election campaigns, initiating legal challenges, and conducting protests or demonstrations. Under certain circumstances, even civil disobedience is a justifiable tactic.

However, we are not suggesting that anything advocacy groups do is acceptable as long as it is within the boundaries of the law. Groups can use any of these forms of intervention to make unsupported allegations, exaggerate the truth, foment tension between social groups, or even advocate violence. We urge advocacy groups to recognize that they occupy a privileged place within our democracy. They are positioned to influence public discourse and citizens' attitudes, and they must acknowledge the responsibilities that accompany this position. Groups should exercise self-restraint in the claims they make, be truthful in their communications with supporters, avoid corrosive personal attacks on opponents and political figures, and acknowledge the need for compromise in a democracy.

Finally, government consultations provide groups with important access to decision makers. Officials who initiate these consultations are usually trying to balance competing interests, so outcomes seldom fully satisfy any of the participants in the process. Groups need to recognize that not all of their concerns can be addressed and that they may need to compromise on some issues. Advocacy groups, particularly those on the losing side of an issue, can become frustrated and disillusioned with the process and may, as a result, eschew future consultations. This means potentially important voices may be lost to these discussions. We therefore encourage groups to continue engaging in consultative processes as long as they believe governments are consulting in good faith.

Recommendations for Governments

Although advocacy groups are essentially private organizations, governments nonetheless play a significant role in supporting advocacy groups, regulating them, and interacting with them through the policy process. In their role as funders and regulators, governments have the capacity to make the Canadian advocacy group system more inclusive of a diversity of societal interests, to encourage organizations to be participatory in their ethos, and to strengthen groups' capacity to encourage citizen participation. In their policy development and implementation roles, governments can establish consultation mechanisms that make them more accessible to input from advocacy groups. They can also create incentives for groups to develop more participatory cultures and be responsive to their constituencies by demonstrating that such values are highly regarded and enhance organizations' credibility. In short, governments can do a great deal to help advocacy groups make positive contributions to the conduct of democracy in Canada.

Government Funding for Advocacy Groups

Throughout this examination of advocacy group organization and activity in Canada, we have noted that lack of money can act as a barrier to the mobilization of groups, to the ability of groups to interact constructively with governments, and to the capacity of groups to operate as internally democratic and inclusive organizations. Chapter 5 discussed in some detail the significant role that the federal government has played in funding advocacy groups in some sectors.

What role should government play in the financing of advocacy groups? An argument could certainly be made that advocacy groups are private organizations and, as such, should fund their activities entirely from private sources. In our view this proposal has three fundamental flaws. First, it fails to recognize that advocacy groups provide public benefit. They provide a channel through which citizens participate in political life, they increase the representative capacity of government by organizing interests, and they bring new information and perspectives to government decision making. All of these activities are in the public interest and warrant some public support. Second, the characterization of advocacy groups as merely private organizations rests on an illusory distinction between the public and the private realm. Other organizations that we once thought of as private organizations – notably political parties and charities – now receive extensive state support. In fact, with the adoption of Bill C-24, An Act to Amend the Canadian Elections Act and Income Tax Act, in 2003, federal political parties are now almost entirely funded by government. Third, if government has a role to play in reducing economic inequity, and we believe it does, then government also has a legitimate role in levelling the playing field for the mobilization of groups whose supporters have fewer financial resources available to them.

At a minimum, government should help advocacy groups help themselves through fundraising. By extending to advocacy groups the tax credit available to registered charities, the federal government would tremendously boost their ability to raise funds from supporters. Even a less generous credit would be an asset to advocacy groups' fundraising efforts. Moreover, such a measure would symbolically recognize the public value placed on advocacy activities.

Allowing advocacy groups to issue tax receipts to donors would also bring them under a federal regulatory framework, although groups that wished to avoid this could simply operate without issuing tax receipts. A regulatory framework would allow government to place some minimum conditions on advocacy groups in order to achieve or maintain their registration status. Such minimum conditions could require that members elect the board of directors of the organization, and that organizations report annually to members on their activities and financial status. Such regulations would not impose an undue burden on most groups, and would signal the value placed on internal accountability and democracy within groups.

We also believe that governments should provide direct assistance to groups that might otherwise be unable to mobilize. As we discussed in some detail in Chapter 5, the federal government's ad hoc approach to funding advocacy groups has had deleterious effects on groups' capacity to organize once funding was withdrawn. Moreover, governments have sometimes tried to use financial support for groups as a method for furthering the government's own policy objectives. Therefore we believe direct funding to groups should not be delivered in the ad hoc manner of the past, and its delivery must be rationally connected to the objective for funding. In our view, the objective for funding advocacy groups is to overcome obstacles to mobilization presented by the following:

- a lack of resources among the population being mobilized
- the diffuse character of the interest in question
- the particular bilingual and geographically dispersed character of Canada.

Government should be involved in funding groups, then, only when they clearly face one of these barriers.

In the past, funding for groups has been delivered through a variety of programs run out of a number of ministries. Allowing government officials to fund the organizations that they then consult with is a practice fraught with difficulties. We propose that government funding for the core operations of advocacy groups should be delivered through an arms-length body that receives predictable funding and is given carte blanche to fund organizations in a manner that furthers the objective outlined above. Funding should be delivered in multiyear, predictable grants. Core funding unrelated to the third barrier should be made contingent on organizations' presentation of plans to become self-supporting over a reasonable period. In short, government should be there to assist groups to overcome barriers to mobilization in their early years, and it should encourage groups to find ways to become sustainable, independent organizations. Some national groups may require funding for translation and travel over the long term, but that is the cost of maintaining viable national organizations in a vast and bilingual country.

These are costly suggestions, although the proposal for funding national organizations could be financed at least in part by centralizing the subsidies to organizations currently offered on an ad hoc basis by various departments. However, the outlay of some public monies is an investment in a vibrant democracy and a recognition of the significance of advocacy organizations to the quality of policy development and decision making in Canada.

Government Regulation of Advocacy Groups and Activities

Although government has a significant role to play in helping advocacy groups to mobilize and raise funds from supporters, we think governments should not be overly intrusive in their efforts to regulate advocacy organizations. Freedom of association and speech are cornerstones of democratic life, and regulation of the activities of the organizations that emerge out of these freedoms should be undertaken only when a compelling public interest is at stake. The examination of advocacy group activities in Chapters 6 and 7 identified three contentious aspects of their regulation: registration of paid lobbyists, third-party election advertising, and limitations on political protest. We will discuss each of these in turn.

Groups, particularly those representing business, hire lobbyists to try to influence government policy. Although we are less than enthusiastic about the practice of hiring lobbyists in order to benefit from their political connections, this practice is almost inevitable in a complex modern democracy. Many paid lobbyists are, in fact, selling expertise and not just influence. That said, the public interest is best served when contacts between lobbyists and government officials are transparent. Citizens will never know what is said behind closed doors during such meetings, but we are at least entitled to know that the meetings took place. The lobbyists' registries in place at the federal level and at the provincial level in Ontario, Nova Scotia, British Columbia, and Quebec go some distance toward achieving this transparency.

In Chapter 6, we outlined the major deficiencies in the Federal Lobbyists Registry, which also apply to provincial registries that are constructed along similar lines. Lobbyists are able to file extraordinarily vague reports about their lobby objectives, compliance is believed to be incomplete, and there is no check on whether lobbyists register. Remedies for these deficiencies are fairly simple. First, when lobbyists register, they should be required to report on precisely what aspect of legislation, regulation, or enforcement they are lobbying. Second, to raise levels of compliance, government officials should also be required to file records of their meetings with lobbyists. This would allow officials from the Lobbyists Registry to check lobbyists' compliance with the law.

As with lobbying, our approach to advocacy groups' interventions in election campaigns relies heavily on transparency. We believe the public interest is best served if there are few limits on advocacy groups' activities in elections, but the public has timely and complete access to the sources of funding for this activity. As noted in Chapter 7, advocacy group advertising in election campaigns can broaden the range of issues discussed in a campaign and can help to focus public attention on policy-related debates at election time. The only restriction necessary is that citizens should know who is paying for advertisements. The source of contributions to groups advertising in election campaigns must therefore be disclosed. Such disclosure is the most meaningful if groups must make the information public *before* election day, not months afterward.

We take a similarly liberal view when it comes to the regulation of political protest. Undoubtedly demonstrators and protesters can create a public inconvenience; when they are protesting in support of a cause one disagrees with, they can be positively infuriating. But ultimately, the right to protest is a bedrock freedom that should not be limited except when public safety is at risk. Chapter 7 outlined what we see as a worrisome trend toward the criminalization of dissent and unnecessary use of force against protesters.

Our recommendations centre on the need for governments to consider the legitimacy of protest in the context of democracy. When protesters gather, police and other officials should try to give them reasonable access to the locations where their protest is directed. Government leaders do not benefit by being shielded from the sight of those who disagree with their policies; democracy benefits even less when this happens. The difficult task of maintaining public safety during political protests is best managed by "soft" policing, at least at the outset. The unnecessary appearance of riot police armed with shields and pepper spray can spark confrontations rather than prevent them. Police forces have learned a great deal in recent years about working with protesters to plan security and about making a nonconfrontational showing at protests. These efforts should be emulated, and confrontational tactics minimized. Most significant, however, is the need to limit the criminalization of dissent. The practices in recent years of arresting leaders of dissenting groups during or prior to protests, and of refusing to allow protesters to cross borders into Canada, do great harm to our democracy. Governments must be vigilant to ensure that police officers, customs officials, and others understand the role of protest in a free and democratic society.

Government Interactions with Groups

We believe that governments develop better public policy when they consult with groups. This does not mean that governments should be puppets of advocacy groups; on the contrary, governments must exercise their capacity as representatives of the entire electorate to make judgments about the merits and legitimacy of advocacy groups' arguments and claims. But governments need to hear these arguments and claims before making decisions.

In general, we believe that governments should try to consult widely with advocacy groups, and to consult early in the policy process so that the resulting inputs have the potential to shape public policy. While not all consultations will take place in the public arena, it is important that at least some do so. The optimal place for these consultations is in legislative committee hearings. These hearings are on the public record, they are open to all groups, and they bring advocacy groups face-to-face with elected officials. We are greatly concerned that many provincial legislatures do not use legislative committees to solicit public input into general policy matters and specific legislation.

We also advocate that when governments are consulting with advocacy groups, they try to discover the group's representative capacity. Government decision makers need to ask explicit questions to group leaders about how many members a group has, what entitlements membership carries, and how policy stances are adopted within a group. By asking these kinds of questions, government decision makers equip themselves to evaluate the representativeness of a group's claim, and also signal to groups the significance government places on participatory and representative advocacy organizations.

Conclusion

If this book has demonstrated one thing, it is that the term "advocacy group" encompasses a tremendously large range of activities and actors. From cigar-chomping lobbyists advocating for the interests of business to Birkenstock-clad citizens organizing to improve the environment, these groups share the common objective of trying to achieve political change. The existence of such a large number and wide variety of groups demonstrates a fundamental strength of Canadian democracy: fundamental freedoms of assembly and speech allow advocacy groups to thrive. In turn, these groups contribute to Canadian democracy by providing a channel through which citizens can voice their preferences, by articulating competing points of view, and by challenging governments to be responsive to citizens.

We are by no means entirely content with the status quo. There is considerable scope for advocacy groups to reform their practices to become more vibrant democratic actors. Advocacy groups could do more to engage citizens in active participation, and governments could do more to support a diverse advocacy group system. Even though we have documented the ability of business interests to dominate in many policy domains, we note with considerable satisfaction that the proliferation of citizens' groups over the past thirty years has introduced something of a counterbalance.

These concerns aside, advocacy groups remain one of the healthier elements of Canadian democracy. They are better adapted to Canadians' changing political values than are more traditional, hierarchical organizations like political parties. Advocacy groups are able to act as dynamic and effective players in the policy process, and citizens are coming to recognize this ability. In an era in which citizens' evaluations of democracy are not positive and many citizens believe they cannot affect government policy, it is essential to strengthen the organizations that citizens do see as an effective means for political engagement: advocacy groups.

Discussion Questions

Chapter 2: Perspectives on Advocacy Groups and Democracy
1 Advocacy groups play a significant role in all established democracies. What is it about these political systems that makes advocacy groups thrive?
2 Review the arguments in this chapter regarding whether advocacy groups contribute to or detract from democracy. Which do you think are the most convincing arguments? Why?
3 Think about an advocacy group you are familiar with. List the ways in which it is contributing to and detracting from democracy.

Chapter 3: Who Participates in Advocacy Groups?
1 Is it fair to say that advocacy groups compensate for the underrepresentation of certain segments of society in mainstream political institutions?
2 Are you, or members of your family, members of any advocacy groups? Why or why not? If you are a member, how active are you?
3 What factors do you think are driving the trend toward chequebook participation in advocacy groups?
4 Why do you think members of advocacy groups are more likely to participate in other political activities? Do you think that their membership in advocacy groups causes this participation, or are these individuals simply more politically active in the first place?

Chapter 4: The Internal Life of Groups
1 What are the pros and cons of having members for advocacy groups?
2 What are "compensatory" groups? What role do "compensatory" groups serve in the Canadian political system?
3 Some advocacy groups use surveys to help determine their organization's policy stance. What are the potential advantages and disadvantages of using this technique?
4 Should we expect advocacy groups to be participatory organizations? Why or why not?

Chapter 5: Which Interests and Identities Are Mobilized?
1 What is the "free rider problem"? What reasons do individuals have not to act as "free riders"?

2 Think of examples of either diffuse interests or segments of society with few resources. How well have they been able to mobilize as advocacy groups? Have they faced barriers to mobilization? How have they overcome these barriers?

3 In your opinion, should governments provide funding for advocacy groups? Why or why not?

4 Should advocacy groups have the same tax status as charities? Why or why not?

Chapter 6: Talking to Governments

1 What restrictions do you think should be placed on paid lobbyists? Why?

2 What types of activities constitute government consultation? What considerations should groups take into account when they decide whether to participate in a consultation process?

3 Compare parliamentary or legislative hearings with private meetings of various stakeholders and government officials. How do these consultative mechanisms measure up against one another?

Chapter 7: Advocacy Group Involvement in Elections, Litigation, and Protests

1 What is meant by "negative" election advertising? Should the targeting of candidates be allowed during election campaigns?

2 Should advocacy groups be limited in their activities during election campaigns? Why or why not?

3 Why might an advocacy group choose to use litigation to achieve the policy outcomes it desires? Is this practice undemocratic?

4 Why do some advocacy groups utilize protest tactics? Can illegal or violent tactics ever be justified? If so, under what conditions?

Chapter 8: Who Prevails?

1 What evidence is there to support the claim that business is privileged in its relationship to government? Is there any evidence that challenges this assumption?

2 Think of a policy issue on which advocacy groups have been active. What factors have determined whether the groups are successful in achieving their policy objectives? What conclusions can you draw from this?

3 How can governments find the right balance between being responsive to organized interests and being captive to them?

Chapter 9: Enhancing the Democratic Role of Advocacy Groups

1 In your opinion, is it reasonable to ask advocacy groups to consider themselves as democratic institutions as well as advocates for a particular cause? Why or why not?

2 Should governments play a role in strengthening advocacy organizations? Why or why not?

3 Evaluate the pros and cons of the proposals for tax credits and government funding of advocacy groups set out in this chapter.

4 How can government decision makers engage in more meaningful interactions with advocacy groups without appearing to be puppets of these organizations? How can groups work more effectively with governments without appearing to betray their principles?

Additional Reading

Chapter 2: Perspectives on Advocacy Groups and Democracy

Robert Dahl's 1961 classic *Who governs?* provides an elegant statement of the pluralist view of interest groups, while E.E. Schattschneider articulates many of the core critiques of the pluralist view in his 1960 work *The semi-sovereign people*. In her article "A deliberative theory of interest representation," political theorist Jane Mansbridge (1992) contributes to this conversation by arguing that interest groups are essential to the kind of deliberative processes that produce sound public policy.

Chapter 3: Who Participates in Advocacy Groups?

The claim that group participation provides citizens with information and skills that are easily transferred to various political activities was first presented in Alexis de Tocqueville's *Democracy in America* ([1831] 1969). It was reintroduced in the 1960s by Gabriel Almond and Sidney Verba's *The civic culture: Political attitudes and democracy in five nations* (1963) and appears again in *Voice and equality: Civic voluntarism in American politics* by Verba, Kay Lehman Schlozman, and Henry Brady (1995). Robert Putnam's more recent argument about the role of social capital (*Bowling alone*, 2000) also emphasizes the role of voluntary organizations in enhancing social trust and leading to a more politically active citizenry. However, important questions have been raised about the benefits of the relationships between groups and their members that are purely financial in nature. See for example William Maloney's "Contracting out the participation function: Social capital and cheque-book participation" (1999) and William Stanbury's *Environmental groups and the international conflict over the forests of British Columbia, 1990-2000* (2000).

Chapter 4: The Internal Life of Groups

Susan Phillips argues in "Redefining government relationships with the voluntary sector: On great expectations and sense and sensibility" (1995) that advocacy groups are often dismissed as "special interests" and their legitimacy is challenged by questions about their ability to reflect concerns of their memberships. Two case studies illustrate some of the arguments about ideal democratic structures of advocacy groups. Miriam Smith's book *Lesbian and gay rights in Canada: Social movements and equality-seeking 1971-1995* (1999) and her article "Segmented networks: Linguistic practices in Canadian lesbian and gay rights organizing" (2004) both provide useful analyses of the gay and lesbian movement in Canada and highlight the challenges that it has faced in developing inclusive, participatory, and responsive structures without financial support from the federal government. Anne Molgat and Joan Grant Cummings's web article "An action that will not be allowed to subside: NAC's first twenty-five years" (2003) and Jill Vickers, Pauline Rankin, and Christine Appelle's book *Politics as if women mattered: A political analysis of the National Action Committee on the Status of Women* (1993) both provide useful histories of the Canadian women's movement and its struggles to develop organizational structures and practices that reflect the democratic value of inclusiveness.

Chapter 5: Which Interests and Identities Are Mobilized?
Mancur Olson's 1965 book *The logic of collective action* presents key arguments for why some interests mobilize and others do not. He introduces the problem of "free riders" — individuals who benefit from the actions of others without themselves engaging in political actions. He also highlights the greater incentives for groups to mobilize around selective versus collective benefits and narrow versus diffuse issues.

The incentives and challenges facing group mobilization are illustrated in case studies of policy areas such as language, multiculturalism, and feminism (Leslie Pal 1993, *Interests of state: The politics of language, multiculturalism and feminism in Canada*), telecommunications (Richard Schultz 2002, *The Consumers Association of Canada and the federal telecommunications regulatory system, 1973-1992*), poverty (Rodney Haddow 1990, "The poverty policy community in Canada's liberal welfare state") and disability issues (William Boyce et al. 2001, *A seat at the table: Persons with disabilities and policy making*).

Arguments surrounding the importance of government's role in facilitating group mobilization can be found in Luc Juillet et al., "The impact of changes in the funding environment on nonprofit organizations" (2001), Paul Pross, *Group politics and public policy* (1992), Susan Phillips, "Redefining government relationships with the voluntary sector: On great expectations and sense and sensibility" (1995), and Miriam Smith, *Lesbian and gay rights in Canada: Social movements and equality-seeking 1971-1995* (1999).

Chapter 6: Talking to Governments
Groups employ different strategies to communicate with governments. Some, such as those discussed in John Sawatsky's 1987 book *The insiders: Government, business and the lobbyists*, hire professional lobby firms to establish contact with government officials. As Paul Pross and Iain Stewart have discussed in their 1993

article "Lobbying, the voluntary sector and the public purse," governments have attempted to regulate these activities in past decades through a Lobbyist's Code of Conduct. Other groups, as Pross and Kernaghan Webb have demonstrated in "Will the walls come tumblin' down? The possible consequences of liberalizing advocacy constraints on charities" (2002), rely on the lobby efforts of grassroot volunteers to pressure legislators, officials, and cabinet ministers. Still others engage in the various types of public consultation outlined by Peter Sterne and Sandra Zagon in *Public consultation guide: Changing the relationship between governments and Canadians* (1997), and by Evert Lindquist in "Citizens, experts and budgets: Evaluating Ottawa's emerging budget process" (1994).

Chapter 7: Advocacy Group Involvement in Elections, Litigation and Protests

R. Kenneth Carty, William Cross, and Lisa Young's book *Rebuilding Canadian party politics* (2000) argues that groups make use of three strategies to influence election campaigns: working on behalf of particular parties, engaging in an issue advocacy campaign, and targeting specific MPs as punishment for their positions on critical group concerns. These strategies are discussed further in Janet Hiebert's chapter "Interest groups and Canadian federal elections" (1991) on third-party advertising on free trade during the 1988 election campaign, and in A. Brian Tanguay and Barry Kay's 1998 article "Third party advertising and the threat to electoral democracy in Canada: The mouse that roared" examining the impact of the National Citizens Coalition's efforts to defeat specific candidates in 1997.

Ted Morton and Rainer Knopff (2000) have argued in their book *The Charter revolution and the court party* that the increased use of litigation by interest groups has weakened Canadian democracy by supplanting elected politicians with unelected and unaccountable judges. In particular, they are concerned with the use of the courts by such groups as linguistic and religious minorities, civil libertarians, feminists, gay and lesbian rights groups, and environmental organizations seeking social change. Gregory Hein's work (2000, *Interest group litigation and Canadian democracy*) makes it clear that litigation is often viewed as a risky endeavour and is considered by groups only as a complement to and not a replacement for traditional lobbying strategies.

Few Canadian studies have been written about the use of protests as a means to raise awareness of advocacy groups' concerns, but Paul Pross and Kernaghan Webb (2002, "Will the walls come tumblin' down? The possible consequences of liberalizing advocacy constraints on charities") report that the rate of protest activity and confidence in the efficacy of protests declined between the early and late 1990s.

Additional Reading

Chapter 8: Who Prevails?

The question of who has influence on government decisions is central to the study of advocacy groups. Robert Presthus's 1973 book *Elite accommodation in Canadian politics* found the Canadian political elite dominated by business and economic interests. Similarly, William Coleman's book *Business and politics: a study of collective action* (1988) argued that there was a systematic bias that resulted in the interests of the business community receiving greater public attention than those of other groups. Alternatively, studies such as Benjamin Cashore et al.'s book *In search of sustainability: British Columbia forest policy* (2001) on the forest industry, Leslie Pal's book *Interests of state: The politics of language, multiculturalism and feminism in Canada* (1993), or Jonathan Malloy's article "What makes a state advocacy structure effective? Conflicts between bureaucratic and social movement criteria" (1999) provide examples of the various conditions under which nonbusiness advocacy groups can succeed. Coleman and Grace Skogstad (1990) provide a theoretically informed discussion about the influence of policy communities and policy networks on public policy in their collection *Policy communities and public policy in Canada*.

Works Cited

Almond, Gabriel, and Sidney Verba. 1963. *The civic culture: Political attitudes and democracy in five nations*. Boston: Little, Brown.

Amara, Nabil, Réjean Landry, and Moktar Lamari. 1999. Les déterminants de l'effort de lobbying des associations au Canada. *Revue Canadienne de science politique* 32(3): 471-98.

Archer, Keith, and Janet Alford. 1997. Activism and representation in an environmental group: The case of the Alberta Wilderness Association. *Southeastern Political Review* 25(1): 133-60.

Billiet, Jaak B., and Bart Cambré. 1999. Social capital, active membership in voluntary associations and some aspects of political participation: An empirical case study. In *Social capital and European democracy*, ed. Jan W. van Deth, Marco Maraffi, Ken Newton, and Paul F. Whiteley, 240-62. London and New York: Routledge.

Boyce, William, Mary Ann McColl, Mary Tremblay, Jerome Bickenbach, Anne Crichton, Steven Andrews, Nancy Gerein, and April D'Aubin. 2001. *A seat at the table: Persons with disabilities and policy making*. Montreal and Kingston: McGill-Queen's University Press.

Bridge, Richard. 2000. *The law of advocacy by charitable organizations: The case for change*. Vancouver: Institute for Media, Policy and Civil Society.

Brooks, Stephen, and Andrew Stritch. 1991. *Business and government in Canada*. Scarborough, ON: Prentice-Hall.

CAA (Canadian Automobile Association). 2003. Statement of policy 2002-2003. <www.caa.ca>. 1 July 2003.

Cairns, Alan. 1985. The embedded state: State-society relations in Canada. In *State and society: Canada in comparative perspective*, ed. Keith G. Banting, 53-86. Toronto: University of Toronto Press.

Canadian Election Study. 2000. <www.fas.umontreal.ca/pol/ces-eec/index.html>. 21 April 2004.

Carty, R. Kenneth, William Cross, and Lisa Young. 2000. *Rebuilding Canadian party politics*. Vancouver: UBC Press.

Cashore, Benjamin, George Hoberg, Michael Howlett, Jeremy Rayner, and Jeremy Wilson. 2001. *In search of sustainability: British Columbia forest policy in the 1990s*. Vancouver: UBC Press.

CCRA (Canada Customs and Revenue Agency). 2003. Registering a charity for income tax purposes. <www.ccra.ca>. 1 July 2003.

CCRC (Canadian Community Reinvestment Coalition). 1997. A financial consumer organization for Canada: Balancing the financial services marketplace. <www.cancrc.org/english/fincomeng.html>. 1 July 2002.

Chekki, Dan A., and Roger T. Toews. 1985. *Organized interest groups and the urban policy process.* Winnipeg: Institute of Urban Studies.

Coleman, William D. 1988. *Business and politics: A study of collective action.* Kingston and Montreal: McGill-Queen's University Press.

—. 1994. Policy convergence in banking: A comparative study. *Political Studies* 42: 274-92.

Coleman, William D., and Grace Skogstad, eds. 1990. *Policy communities and public policy in Canada.* Mississauga, ON: Copp Clark Pitman.

Collier, Cheryl. 2001. Working with parties: Success and failure of child care advocates in British Columbia and Ontario in the 1990s. In *Changing child care: Five decades of child care advocacy and policy in Canada,* ed. Susan Prentice, 117-31. Halifax: Fernwood Publishing.

Commission for Public Complaints Against the RCMP. 2002. Chair's final report. <www.cpc-cpp.gc.ca/ePub/APEC/eFinalApec.pdf>. 1 July 2003.

Council of Canadians. 2003. Annual general meeting, 24-6 October 2003. Unpublished document. Vancouver.

Cross, William. 2004. *Political parties.* Vancouver: UBC Press.

Curtis, James E., Edward Grabb, and Douglas Baer. 1992. Voluntary association membership in fifteen countries. *American Sociological Review* 57(1): 139-52.

Curtis, Jenefer. 2003. Lobbyist handlers extraordinaire. *Hill Times* (Ottawa), May 19.

Dahl, Robert A. 1961. *Who governs?* New Haven: Yale University Press.

Dalton, Russell. 1988. *Citizen politics in Western democracies: Public opinion and political parties in the United States, Great Britain, West Germany and France.* Chatham, NJ: Chatham House.

Dekker, Paul, and Andries van den Broek. 1996. Volunteering and politics: Involvement in voluntary associations from a "civic culture" perspective. In *Political value change in Western democracies,* ed. Loek Halman and Neil Nevitte, 125-49. Tilburg, Netherlands: Tilburg University Press.

—. 1998. Civil Society in comparative perspective: Involvement in voluntary associations in North America and Western Europe. *Voluntas* 1: 11-38.

Democracy Watch. 1997. Democracy Watch criticizes lack of access for consumer groups to minister responsible for Bank Act changes. Media release. <www. dwatch.ca/camp/bnkopConsum98.html>.

Docherty, David. 2004. *Legislatures.* Vancouver: UBC Press.

Embuldeniya, Don K. 2001. *Exploring the health, strength and impact of Canada's civil society.* Toronto: Canadian Centre for Philanthropy.

Falconer, Tim. 2001. *Watchdogs and gadflies: Activism from marginal to mainstream*. Toronto: Penguin/Viking.

Finkle, Peter, Kernaghan Webb, William T. Stanbury, and Paul Pross. 1994. Federal government relations with interest groups: A reconsideration. Discussion paper prepared for the Consumer Policy Framework Secretariat, Consumer and Corporate Affairs Canada. Ottawa: Government of Canada.

Fletcher, Wendy. 1994. Child care interest groups in Alberta. MA thesis, University of Calgary.

Fortier, Isabelle, Eric Montpetit, and Francesca Scala. 2003. Democratic practices vs. expertise: The National Action Committee on the Status of Women and Canada's policy on reproductive technology. Paper presented at the annual meeting of the Canadian Political Science Association, Halifax, 30 May-1 June 2003.

Fullerton, Robin. 1995. Retaining state hegemony in Canada in the 1990s: Government response to an agricultural disaster. *Canadian Review of Sociology and Anthropology* 32(1): 53-67.

Gidengil, Elisabeth, André Blais, Neil Nevitte, and Richard Nadeau. 2004. *Citizens.* Vancouver: UBC Press.

Goodwin, R.K. 1988. *One billion dollars of influence*. Chatham House, NJ: Chatham House.

Greene, Ian. 2005. *The courts*. Vancouver: UBC Press.

Haddow, Rodney. 1990. The poverty policy community in Canada's liberal welfare state. In *Policy communities and public policy in Canada,* ed. William D. Coleman and Grace Skogstad, 212-37. Toronto: Copp Clark Pitman.

Hein, Gregory. 1997. Social movements and the expansion of judicial power: Feminists and environmentalists in Canada from 1970 to 1995. Ph.D. diss., University of Toronto.

—. 2000. *Interest group litigation and Canadian democracy*. Montreal: Institute for Research in Public Policy.

Hiebert, Janet. 1991. Interest groups and Canadian federal elections. In *Interest groups and elections in Canada,* ed. F. Leslie Seidle, 3-76. Toronto: Dundurn Press.

Howe, R. Brian, and David Johnson. 1995. Variations in enforcing equality: A study of provincial human rights funding. *Canadian Public Administration* 38(2): 242-62.

Howe, Paul, and David Northrup. 2000. Strengthening Canadian democracy survey. Institute for Research in Public Policy.

Johnston, Richard, André Blais, Henry E. Brady, and Jean Crete. 1992. *Letting the people decide: Dynamics of a Canadian election*. Montreal and Kingston: McGill-Queen's University Press.

Juillet, Luc, Caroline Andrew, Tim Aubry, and Janet Mrenica. 2001. The impact of changes in the funding environment on nonprofit organizations. In *The nonprofit sector and government in a new century*, ed. Kathy L. Brock and Keith G. Banting, 21-62. Montreal and Kingston: McGill-Queen's University Press.

Kobayashi, Audrey. 2000. Advocacy from the margins: The role of minority ethnocultural associations in affecting public policy in Canada. In *The nonprofit sector in Canada: Roles and relationships*, ed. Keith Banting, 229-61. Kingston, ON: Queen's University School of Policy Studies.

Kobrin, Stephen J. 1998. The MAI and the clash of globalizations. *Foreign Policy* 112: 97-110.

KPMG Consulting. 2001. *Study on compliance under the Lobbyists Registration Act: Final report*.

Kruzynski, Anna K., and Eric Shragge. 1999. Getting organized: Anti-poverty organizing and social citizenship in the 1970s. *Community Development Journal* 34(3): 328-39.

Laghi, Brian, and Daniel Leblanc. 2002. Donations to Liberals hit $15.9 million. *Globe and Mail*, 4 July, A6.

Langford, Tom. 2001. From social movement to marginalized interest groups: Advocating for quality child care in Alberta, 1965-86. In *Changing child care: Five decades of child care advocacy and policy in Canada*, ed. Susan Prentice, 63-79. Halifax: Fernwood Publishing.

Lindblom, Charles E. 1963. *The intelligence of democracy*. New York: Free Press.

Lindquist, Evert A. 1994. Citizens, experts and budgets: Evaluating Ottawa's emerging budget process. In *How Ottawa spends 1994-95: Making change*, ed. Susan D. Phillips, 91-128. Ottawa: Carleton University Press.

Lindquist, Evert A., and David M. Rayside. 1992. Federal AIDS policy for the 1990s: Is it too early for mainstreaming in Canada? In *How Ottawa spends: The politics of competitiveness*, ed. Frances Abele, 313-52. Ottawa: Carleton University Press.

Lowi, Theodore. 1979. *The end of liberalism*. New York: Free Press.

Lyons, Tom, and Bruce Livesey. 2001. Uncovering the undercovers: How and why Toronto's police intelligence unit spies on activists. *Eye* (Toronto), 18 January. <www.eye.net/eye/issue/issue_01.18.01/news/cops.html>. 1 July 2002.

Macdonald, Douglas. 2003. The business campaign to prevent Kyoto ratification. Paper presented to the annual meeting of the Canadian Political Science Association, Dalhousie University, 31 May.

Madison, James. [1778] 1966. *Federalist Papers.* New Rochelle, NY: Arlington House.

Malloy, Jonathan. 1999. What makes a state advocacy structure effective? Conflicts between bureaucratic and social movement criteria. *Governance* 12(3): 267-88.

Maloney, William A. 1999. Contracting out the participation function: Social capital and cheque-book participation. In *Social capital and European democracy,* ed. Jan W. van Deth, Marco Maraffi, Ken Newton, and Paul F. Whiteley, 108-19. London and New York: Routledge.

Maloney, William, and Grant Jordan. 1997. Mobilization and participation in large-scale campaigning in Britain: The rise of protest businesses in Britain. In *Private groups and public life: Social participation, voluntary association, and political involvement in representative democracies,* ed. Jan W. van Deth, 107-24. London: Routledge.

Maloney, William A., Graham Smith, and Gerry Stoker. 2000. Social capital and associational life. In *Social capital: Critical perspectives,* ed. Stephen Baran, John Field, and Tom Schuller, 212-25. Oxford: Oxford University Press.

Mansbridge, Jane. 1992. A deliberative theory of interest representation. In *The politics of interests: Interest groups transformed,* ed. Mark P. Petracca, 32-57. Boulder, CO: Westview Press.

Mill, John Stuart. [1861] 1972. *Utilitarianism, On liberty and considerations on representative government.* London: J.M. Dent & Sons Ltd.

Molgat, Anne, and Joan Grant Cummings. 2003. An action that will not be allowed to subside: NAC's first twenty-five years. <www.nac-cca.ca/about/his_e.htm>. 1 July 2003.

Montpetit, Eric. 2003a. Public consultations in policy network environments: The case of assisted reproductive technology policy in Canada. *Canadian Public Policy* 29(1): 95-110.

—. 2003b. Policy networks, federalism and managerial ideas: How ART non-decision in Canada safeguards the autonomy of the medical profession. In *Comparative biomedical policy: Governing assisted reproductive technologies,* ed. I. Bleiklie, M. Goggin, and C. Rothmayr, 64-82. London: Routledge.

Morton, F.L., and Rainer Knopff. 2000. *The Charter revolution and the court party.* Peterborough, ON: Broadview Press.

Moyser, George, and Geraint Parry. 1997. Voluntary associations and democratic participation in Britain. In *Private groups and public life,* ed. Jan W. van Deth, 26-46. London: Routledge.

Nevitte, Neil. 1996. *The decline of deference.* Peterborough, ON: Broadview Press.

Newman, Peter C. 1998. *Titans: How the new Canadian establishment seized power.* Toronto: Penguin.

OCAP (Ontario Coalition Against Poverty). 2002. A short history of OCAP. <www. ocap.ca/dispatch.cgi/archive/Short_History_of_OCAP>. 1 July 2002.

Olsen, Marvin. 1972. Social participation and voting turnout: A multivariate analysis. *American Sociological Review* 37: 317-22.

Olson, Mancur. 1965. *The logic of collective action.* New York: Schocken.

Pal, Leslie A. 1993. *Interests of state: The politics of language, multiculturalism and feminism in Canada.* Montreal and Kingston: McGill-Queen's University Press.

Phillips, Susan. 1995. Redefining government relationships with the voluntary sector: On great expectations and sense and sensibility. <www.vsr-trsb.net/ publications/phillips-e.html>.

Phillips, Susan, with Michael Orsini. 2002. *Mapping the links: citizen involvement in policy processes.*CPRN Discussion Paper No. F/21. Ottawa: Canadian Policy Research Networks. <www.cprn.org>. 1 July 2002.

PPF (Public Policy Forum). 2001. *Bridging two solitudes: A discussion paper on federal government-industry relations.* Ottawa: Public Policy Forum.

Presthus, Robert. 1973. *Elite accommodation in Canadian politics.* Cambridge: Cambridge University Press.

Pross, A. Paul. 1992. *Group politics and public policy.* 2nd ed. Toronto: Oxford University Press.

Pross, A. Paul, and Iain S. Stewart. 1993. Lobbying, the voluntary sector and the public purse. In *How Ottawa spends 1993-4: A more democratic Canada?* ed. Susan D. Phillips, 109-42. Ottawa: Carleton University Press.

—. 1994. Breaking the habit: Attentive publics and tobacco regulation. In *How Ottawa spends 1994-95: Making change,* ed. Susan D. Phillips, 129-64. Ottawa: Carleton University Press.

Pross, A. Paul, and Kernaghan R. Webb. 2002. Will the walls come tumblin' down? The possible consequences of liberalizing advocacy constraints on charities. Paper presented at Queen's University Conference on the Third Sector, Kingston, ON, 25-6 October.

Pue, Wesley. 2000. Policing, the rule of law and accountability in Canada: Lessons from the APEC summit. In *Pepper in our eyes: The APEC affair,* ed. Wesley Pue, 3-26. Vancouver: UBC Press.

Putnam, Robert. 1993. *Making democracy work: Civic traditions in modern Italy.* Princeton: Princeton University Press.

—. 1995. Bowling alone: America's declining social capital. *Journal of Democracy* 6(1): 65-78.

—. 2000. *Bowling alone.* New York: Simon and Schuster.

Rathjen, Heidi, and Charles Montpetit. 1999. *December 6: From the Montreal massacre to gun control — The inside story.* Toronto: McClelland and Stewart.

Receptions show Alberta needs lobby registry. 2003. *Edmonton Journal,* March 29, A18.

Rosenau, Pauline Vaillancourt. 1994. Impact of political structures and informal political processes on health policy: Comparison of the United States and Canada. *Policy Studies Review* 13(3/4): 293-314.

Sawatsky, John. 1987. *The insiders: Government, business and the lobbyists.* Toronto: McClelland and Stewart.

Schattschneider, E.E. 1960. *The semi-sovereign people.* New York: Holt, Rinehart and Winston.

Schultz, Richard J. 2002. *The Consumers' Association of Canada and the federal telecommunications regulatory system, 1973-1992.* Vancouver: SFU-UBC Centre for the Study of Government and Business.

Sheldrick, Ron M. 1998. Welfare reform under Ontario's NDP: Social democracy and social group representation. *Studies in Political Economy* 55: 37-63.

Smith, Miriam. 1999. *Lesbian and gay rights in Canada: Social movements and equality-seeking, 1971-1995.*Toronto: University of Toronto Press.

—. 2004. Segmented networks: Linguistic practices in Canadian lesbian and gay rights organizing. *Ethnicities* 4(1): 99-124.

Stanbury, W.T. 1986. *Business-government relations in Canada.* Toronto: Methuen.

—. 2000. *Environmental groups and the international conflict over the forests of British Columbia, 1990-2000.* Vancouver: SFU-UBC Centre for the Study of Government and Business.

Sterne, Peter, with Sandra Zagon. 1997. *Public consultation guide: Changing the relationship between governments and Canadians.* Ottawa: Canadian Centre for Management Development.

Tanguay, A. Brian. 2001. Parties, organized interests and electoral democracy: The 1999 Ontario provincial election. In *Political parties, representation and electoral democracy in Canada,* ed. William Cross. Toronto: Oxford University Press.

Tanguay, A. Brian, and Barry J. Kay. 1998. Third party advertising and the threat to electoral democracy in Canada: The mouse that roared. *International Journal of Canadian Studies* 17: 57-79.

Thorburn, Hugh. 1985. *Interest groups in the Canadian federal system.* Toronto: University of Toronto Press.

Tocqueville, Alexis de. [1831] 1969. *Democracy in America*. New York: Doubleday.

Truman, David B. 1951. *The governmental process*. New York: Alfred A. Knopf.

Verba, Sidney, and Norman H. Nie. 1972. *Participation in America: Political democracy and social equality*. New York: Harper and Row.

Verba, Sidney, Kay Lehman Schlozman, and Henry E. Brady. 1995. *Voice and equality: Civic voluntarism in American politics*. Cambridge: Harvard University Press.

Vickers, Jill. 1998. The new politics in Ontario in the 1990s: Protests and movements versus parties. Paper presented to the 1998 Annual Meeting of the Canadian Political Science Association, Ottawa, 31 May-2 June.

Vickers, Jill, Pauline Rankin, and Christine Appelle. 1993. *Politics as if women mattered: A political analysis of the National Action Committee on the Status of Women*. Toronto: University of Toronto Press.

Warby, Michael. 1999. Ambush in cyberspace: NGOs, the Internet and the MAI. *IPA Review* 51(2): 3-5.

Webb, Kernaghan, and Lynda Cassells. 1995. *Coordinating and communicating: A proposed Canadian consumer network*. Ottawa: Office of Consumer Affairs, Industry Canada.

Webb, Kernaghan, Jean-Baptiste Renaud, Karen Ellis, and Derek Ireland. 1996. *Strategic alliances for consumer groups*. Ottawa: Office of Consumer Affairs, Industry Canada.

White, Graham. 2005. *Cabinets and first ministers*. Vancouver: UBC Press.

World Values Survey. Various years. <www.worldvaluessurvey.org>. 21 April 2004.

Young, Lisa, and William Cross. 2003. Women's participation in Canadian political parties. In *Women and electoral politics in Canada,* ed. Manon Tremblay and Linda Trimble, 92-109. Toronto: Oxford University Press.

INDEX

A master index to all volumes in the Canadian Democratic Audit series can be found at www.ubcpress.ca/readingroom/audit/index.

Printed and bound in Canada by Friesens

Copy editor: Sarah Wight

Text Design: Peter Ross, Counterpunch

Typesetter: Artegraphica Design Co. Ltd.

Proofreader: Tara Tovell

Indexer: Patricia Buchanan